Listening for Bas

All Year 'Ro

by Brenda Brumbaugh and Nan Thompson-Trenta

Skills	Ages
■ concepts ■ listening	■ 5 through 8
	Grades
	■ K through 3

Evidence-Based Practice

- Students need to understand semantic connections among words. It may be necessary to target understanding of basic concepts that underpin the vocabulary required to access the curriculum (Taylor-Goh, 2005).
- In-depth knowledge of word meaning helps students comprehend what they read and helps them use words accurately in speaking and reading (Taylor-Goh, 2005).
- Students who struggle with vocabulary acquisition need more trials than typical language learners to maximize vocabulary growth (Montgomery, 2007).
- A systematic approach to teaching vocabulary, including direct and indirect instruction, teaches students that vocabulary is important for learning language and for reading (Beck, McKeown, & Kucan, 2002).
- Klein and Freitag (1991) found that instructional games enhance the motivation of students in the areas of attention, relevance, confidence, and satisfaction, without sacrificing performance.
- Impairment in the ability to comprehend concepts will negatively affect communication and should be targeted for intervention (ASHA, 2000).

Listening for Basic Concepts All Year 'Round incorporates these principles and is also based on expert professional practice.

References

American Speech-Language-Hearing Association (ASHA). (2000). *Guidelines for roles and responsibilities of the school-based speech-language pathologist.* Retrieved March 16, 2010, from www.asha.org/docs/pdf/GL2000-00053.pdf

Beck, I.L., McKeown, M.G., & Kucan, L. (2002). *Bringing words to life: Robust vocabulary instruction.* New York: Guilford Press.

Klein, J.D., & Freitag, E. (1991). Effects of using an instructional game on motivation and performance. *Journal of Educational Research, 84*(5), 303-308.

Montgomery, J. (2007, November). *Vocabulary interventions for RTI: Tiers 1, 2, 3.* Paper presented at the American Speech-Language-Hearing Association Convention, Boston: MA.

Taylor-Goh, S. (2005). *Royal college of speech & language therapists clinical guidelines.* United Kingdom: Speechmark.

LinguiSystems

LinguiSystems, Inc.
3100 4th Avenue
East Moline, IL 61244

800-776-4332

FAX: 800-577-4555
Email: service@linguisystems.com
Web: linguisystems.com

Printed in the U.S.A.

ISBN 10: 1-55999-108-9
ISBN 13: 978-1-55999-108-7

About the Authors

Brenda Brumbaugh, M.A., CCC is a speech-language pathologist for the Perry Local School System in Massillon, Ohio. She works with children from preschool through high school ages who have communication disorders.

Nan Thompson-Trenta, M.A. is also a speech-language pathologist for the Perry Local School System in Massillon, Ohio. She works with children from kindergarten through high school ages who have communication disorders.

Listening for Basic Concepts All Year 'Round is Brenda and Nan's first publication with LinguiSystems.

August 1990

Dedication

From Brenda to her husband, Dennis, and to her parents, David and Norma Swanson, for their loving support

From Nan to her parents, Ray and Annie Thompson, for their loving support

Acknowledgments

We wish to acknowledge the classroom teachers in the Perry Schools who gave us their support and Kathy Nichols for her encouragement.

Table of Contents

Introduction

Several years ago, our kindergarten teachers expressed a need for classroom language and listening lessons. We decided our mission was to fill this need by creating something fun and unique our teachers and children would love. After researching the kindergarten language arts curriculum, we came up with a list of basic language concepts taught at that level. We arranged the concepts in order of difficulty; designed fun stories, creative worksheets, and periodic checks to teach and reinforce these concepts; and created friendly parent letters. We put everything together in a nice, neat package, and voilá...*Listening for Basic Concepts All Year 'Round*!

Listening for Basic Concepts All Year 'Round provides language instructors with a series of fun weekly lessons that build children's understanding of basic concepts through good listening. The listening activities will capture your children's hearts and attention!

Each month of the school year covers four or five concepts, beginning with the easier concepts in September and finishing with the more difficult concepts in May. At the end of each month is a letter and worksheet you can give to the children's parents. The letter lets parents know what concepts you've been working on and gives them a fun exercise to do with their children to reinforce these new concepts. At the end of each three months is a Concept Check. Use these periodic checks to check on your children's progress and retention of new concepts. Your children will enjoy seeing how many new concepts they've learned as they decorate their worksheets.

You'll find a variety of listening activities throughout the year, from listening to stories to listening for worksheet directions to playing Simon Says. Most of the activities require very little preparation and are ready to teach. Many exercises require the children to color on the worksheets provided. In most of these cases, children need a box of eight crayons to complete the exercises. We recommend that you read the instructions for these worksheets aloud twice to insure that your children have a chance to hear everything you say. Also, we choose a good listener in each class every week to be presented with a special award. This award is a great motivator!

Listening for Basic Concepts All Year 'Round has delightful art you and your children will love. You'll soon begin to recognize a familiar character appearing on many of the pages — Brennan Bear. We encourage you to address these lessons with enthusiasm, imagination, and creativity. Have fun with Brennan!

Brenda and Nan

Brennan Goes to School

Directions: Encourage the children to listen carefully as you read the story below. After you read the story, ask the children the questions listed at the bottom of the page.

* * * * * * * * * * * * * * * * * * *

It was Brennan's first day of school and he was very excited! He had heard from his friends how much fun it is to go to school. Brennan stood next to his mother and gave her a big hug. "Bye, Mom," he said with a smile as he walked away from her. He began his walk to school.

On his way to school, Brennan saw a lot of neat things. He saw a bunch of flowers growing next to a tree. He stuck his nose into the flowers and took a big sniff. Buzz, buzz, buzz...out came a bee! "Get away from me, old bee!" cried Brennan.

Then, Brennan smelled a bad smell. He saw an animal standing next to the tree. The animal was black with a white stripe. It was a skunk! Phew! Brennan didn't want to be next to the skunk, so he walked away from it as quickly and quietly as he could.

Brennan was almost to the school when he spotted his friends standing next to someone he didn't know. "Who could that be?" wondered Brennan. As Brennan got closer, all his friends said "Hi, Brennan." Brennan's best friend, Bernie, said, "Brennan, this is our new teacher, Ms. Miller."

"Hello, Brennan," said Ms. Miller with a smile. "I know we're going to have a wonderful year!"

Brennan smiled his biggest bear smile and thought, "Yes, this is going to be a wonderful year!"

Questions:

1. Why was Brennan excited?
2. What did Brennan give his mom before he left for school?
3. What was the first thing Brennan saw on his way to school?
4. Where were the flowers growing?
5. How did Brennan know there was a skunk nearby?
6. What did Brennan do as soon as he saw the skunk?
7. Who did Brennan see when he got to school?
8. Tell why we hug people.
9. Why didn't Brennan want the bee next to him?
10. How can you show someone you're happy?

Back to School: Instructions

Give each child a copy of *Back to School.* Have the children listen carefully and follow your directions. Remind them to listen for the words *next to* and *away from*.

1. Color the flowers next to the house blue.
2. Draw some grass away from the school.
3. Draw two blue clouds next to the sun.
4. Color the bear away from the house brown.
5. Color the flowers away from the house red.
6. Draw a yellow bee next to one of the flowers.
7. Color the tree away from the school green.
8. Draw a bluebird in the tree next to the school.
9. Draw an orange butterfly away from the sun.
10. Draw a black stick next to Brennan.
11. Color the grass next to the house green.
12. Draw another tree away from the school.
13. Draw a pile of yellow and orange leaves next to the path.
14. Draw a flower next to one of the trees.
15. Draw a puddle of water away from the path.

What a nice day for Brennan to go to school!

Back to School

Name ______________________

September: *next to, away from*

A Day at the Farm

Directions: Encourage the children to listen carefully as you read the story below. After you read the story, ask the children the questions listed at the bottom of the page.

✹ ✹ ✹ ✹ ✹ ✹ ✹ ✹ ✹ ✹ ✹ ✹ ✹ ✹ ✹ ✹ ✹ ✹ ✹

Brennan was visiting his Uncle Louie's farm. "I love going to the farm," said Brennan. "There's always so much to see. Each time I come, I see something different in the fields and around the farm. I wonder what I'll see today."

As Brennan walked around the barn, he saw a fat pig lying in the mud. "That pig sure is dirty," exclaimed Brennan. "I don't think I've ever seen him clean. I wonder if he ever gets out of the mud!"

Next, Brennan saw a small white duck swimming in the pond. Her three little ducklings were out of the pond. They were afraid to go in the water. They were having fun waddling around the pond playing follow the leader. Brennan walked closer to the ducklings, but the mother duck quickly got out of the water and started quacking at Brennan to stay away from her little ducklings.

Brennan also saw some cows standing outside the barn, eating grass. They looked very happy. Then, one by one, they slowly went in the barn. "It must be feeding time," thought Brennan.

Next, Brennan saw the dog, Pepper. She was behind her doghouse. Brennan walked over to her and scratched her behind the ears. She really liked that!

The last thing Brennan saw on his walk around the farm was a nest in a big oak tree. There weren't any birds in the nest! Brennan smiled as he walked back to where he had started his walk.

"This was a fun day at the farm," said Brennan. "I'm glad Uncle Louie lives on a farm and has a lot of animals. Maybe I can come to visit again next month."

Questions:

1. Where was Brennan visiting?
2. Why did Brennan like to go to his uncle's farm?
3. What animals did Brennan see?
4. Why didn't the ducklings go in the water?
5. What were the cows doing?
6. Tell how many birds were in the nest.
7. Where do you think the mother bird was?
8. Why do you think Pepper liked to be scratched behind her ears?
9. Name some animals you probably wouldn't find on a farm.
10. What is your favorite farm animal? Why?

Uncle Louie's Farm: Instructions

Give each child a copy of *Uncle Louie's Farm*. Have the children listen carefully and follow your directions. Remind them to listen for the words *in* and *out*.

1. Color the duck in the pond yellow.
2. Draw a bluebird out of the nest.
3. Circle the dog in the doghouse with a brown crayon.
4. Put a purple X on the cow out of the barn.
5. Color the frog out of the pond brown.
6. Color the pig in the mud black.
7. Color the hay in the barn yellow.
8. Color the dog out of the doghouse black.
9. Draw a red apple that has fallen out of the tree.
10. Draw a brown snake in the grass.
11. Color the ducklings out of the pond orange.
12. Draw a brown baby bird in the nest.
13. Color the frog in the pond green.
14. Circle the pig out of the mud with a red crayon.
15. Draw a yellow sun in the sky.

Uncle Louie sure has a lot of animals on his farm!

Uncle Louie's Farm

Name ______________________

Brennan Says

Directions: Have the children line up in the room or outside. Explain that you're going to play a game of "Brennan Says." To play the game, the children must listen to your directions and do only what Brennan says, not what anyone else says. Tell them to listen carefully so they're not tricked! (You may want to practice a few commands before you begin the real thing.)

For additional practice, have the children make up commands using the words *forward* and *backward*. Remind the children to use Brennan's name and other people's names when they give their commands.

1. Brennan says, "Take one step forward."
2. Brennan says, "Take two steps backward."
3. Rodney says, "Hop forward two times."
4. Brennan says, "Crawl backward."
5. Bernie says, "Bend backward."
6. Kim says, "Bend forward."
7. Brennan says, "Hop forward three times."
8. Brennan says, "March backward."
9. Brennan says, "Skip forward."
10. Sam says, "Skip backward."
11. Brennan says, "Stretch your arms forward."
12. Brennan says, "Take one giant step backward."
13. Brett says, "Walk backward three steps."
14. Brennan says, "Walk forward two steps."
15. Chuck says, "Hop backward on one foot."
16. Tim says, "Tiptoe forward."
17. Brennan says, "Hop forward on one foot."
18. Brennan says, "Take one giant step backward."
19. Lavonne says, "March forward."
20. Brennan says, "Tiptoe forward."

Bend Over: Instructions

Give each child a copy of *Bend Over*. Have the children listen carefully and follow your directions. Remind them to listen for the words *forward* and *backward*.

1. Find the bear bending forward. Color his shirt red.
2. Find the bear bending backward. Color his pants blue.
3. Give the bear bending forward yellow shoes.
4. Give the bear bending backward a pair of black glasses.
5. Draw an orange flower under the backward bear.
6. Draw a purple kite above the forward bear.
7. Find the backward bear. Color his shoes brown.
8. Color the forward bear's mouth red.
9. Give the bear bending backward a blue-striped shirt.
10. Put a yellow hat on the bear bending forward.
11. Put a brown baseball bat in front of the bear bending forward.
12. Color the bear's face brown that's bending backward.
13. Use a black crayon to color the paws of the bear bending forward.
14. Find the forward bear. Color his pants green.
15. Draw three black buttons on the shirt of the bear bending backward.

These bears must be in great shape from bending over!

Bend Over

Name ______________________

September: *forward, backward*

Never and *Always* Questions

Directions: Ask the children the following questions. Tell them to listen carefully for the words *never* and *always*. When you're done, have the children make up *never* and *always* questions for each other.

1. Which can you always eat, an apple or a spoon?
2. Name something that's always hot.
3. What can you never wear?
4. Which is always tall, a giraffe or a lamb?
5. What can you never see in the sky?
6. What always has wheels?
7. Name something you would never write with.
8. What is always soft?
9. Name something you would never play with.
10. Where can you always see animals?
11. What would you never see in school?
12. Which can you never throw, a baseball or the moon?
13. Name something that is always small.
14. Which is never sweet, a lemon or an apple?
15. What always lives in water?
16. Name something that never floats.
17. What can you always find in a library?
18. Which will never grow, an oven or a seed?
19. Name something you would never see in a tree house.
20. Where can you always find people who are sick?

Never and *Always*: Instructions

Give each child a copy of *Never* and *Always*. Have the children listen carefully and follow your directions. Remind them to listen for the words *never* and *always*.

1. Look at row one. Use your red crayon to color something you can always eat.
2. Look at row two. Put green circles around the things you never see on a farm.
3. Look at row three. Put a black X on the thing you should never play with.
4. Look at row four. Draw a blue line on something that's always cold.
5. Look at row five. Put a brown circle around something that always grows on a vine.
6. Look at row six. Use your orange crayon to color the thing that never flies.
7. Look at row seven. Put a red circle around the thing that never hops.
8. Look at row eight. Put a purple X on the things you always find in a kitchen.

Good listening!

Never and Always

Name ______________________

1.   

2.   

3.   

4.   

5.   

6.   

7.   

8.   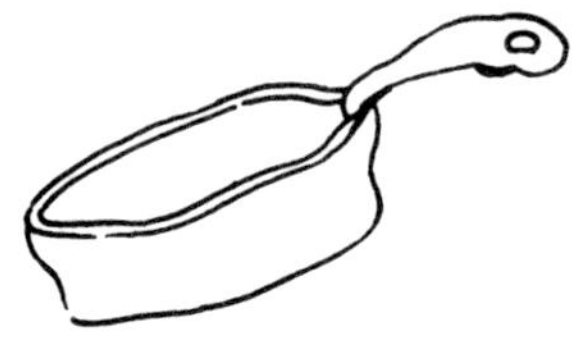

Home Lesson

Dear ______________________ ,

During the month of September, we have been working on these concepts: *next to, away from, in, out, forward, backward, never*, and *always*. You can help your child review these concepts by giving your child the sheet attached to this page. Read the directions below and encourage your child to listen carefully and follow your directions. Here are the materials you will need: a box of eight crayons, a table, a chair, and a quiet place to work.

Directions:

1. Look at row one.

   Color the cheerleader bending backward red.
   Color the cheerleader bending forward blue.

2. Look at row two.

   Use a yellow crayon to color the things you never use to play football.
   Use a brown crayon to color the things you always use to play football.

3. Look at row three.

   Put a purple circle around the school with children in it.
   Put a green X on the school with children coming out of it.

4. Look at row four.

   Use an orange crayon to color the helmet next to the whistle.
   Use a purple crayon to color the helmet away from the whistle.

5. Look at row five.

   Use a yellow crayon to circle the football players facing backward.
   Use a black crayon to circle the football players facing forward.

6. Look at row six.

   Color the leaves away from the tree orange.
   Color the leaves next to the tree green.

Thank you for your help!

Sincerely,

____

Name ______________________

1.   

2.     

3.  

4. 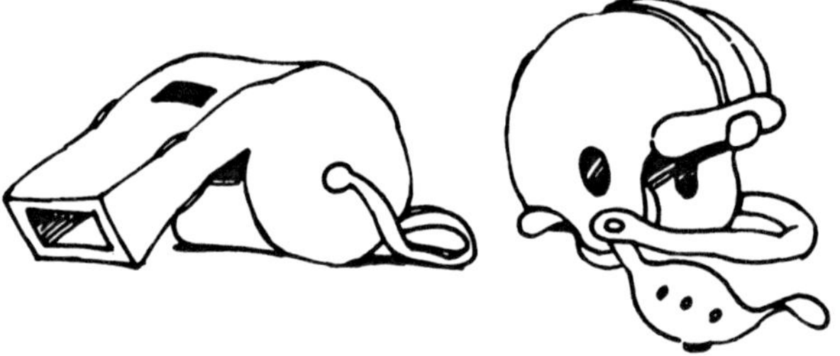 

5.    

6.  

Brennan Visits Bernie

Directions: Give a copy of the following two pages to each child. Then, encourage the children to listen carefully as you read the story below. Each time you say one of the bear's names, have the children hold up the right bear. After you read the story, ask the children the questions listed at the bottom of the page and let the children color their pictures of Brennan and Bernie.

October

* * * * * * * * * * * * * * * * * * *

It was Saturday morning. Brennan Bear watched all his favorite cartoons on TV. Then, he decided to go over to his friend's house. His friend's name was Bernie.

As Brennan walked up the sidewalk to Bernie's house, he saw Bernie coming out the door. "Gee, Bernie," Brennan said. "We look the same today."

"What do you mean?" asked Bernie.

"We're wearing the same baseball caps. They're both blue and have the letter 'B' on them," answered Brennan.

"You're right," said Bernie. "And our jeans are the same, too. They're blue with two pockets."

"Look!" said Brennan. "Our belts are the same, too. They're both brown with gold buckles."

"Oops!" said Bernie. "Not everything is the same. Our shirts are not the same. My shirt has four buttons and yours doesn't have any. Our shoes are not the same, either. Yours are white and mine are brown."

"My shirt has short sleeves and your shirt has long sleeves. That's another way we are not the same," said Brennan. "Oh, well. I guess I should say we almost look the same!"

Questions:

1. What was Brennan doing before he decided to go to his friend's house?
2. Who did Brennan visit?
3. Why did Brennan say that he and Bernie looked the same?
4. Tell how Brennan and Bernie were not the same.
5. Why do you think both baseball caps had the letter "B" on them?
6. What do you like to do when you go to a friend's house?
7. How are you and Brennan the same?
8. Sometimes twins wear clothes that look the same. Would you like to always look the same as your brother or sister? Why or why not?
9. Describe something you're wearing that looks the same as someone else's.
10. Look what I'm wearing. Tell how you are not the same as me.

Brennan

Name ______________________

Bernie

Name ______________________

School Daze: Instructions

Give each child a copy of *School Daze*. Have the children listen carefully and follow your directions. Remind them to listen for the words *same* and *not the same*.

Look at box one.

1. Draw a blue line under the thing that is not the same.
2. Draw green circles around the things that are the same.

Look at box two.

1. Draw a yellow line under each book that is the same.
2. Color the book that is not the same purple.

Look at box three.

1. Put an orange X on the ball that is not the same.
2. Draw a blue circle around the balls that are the same.

Look at box four.

1. Color the papers that are the same red.
2. Put a yellow X on the paper that is not the same.

Look at box five.

1. Draw a green square around the scissors that are not the same.
2. Color the scissors that are the same brown.

Look at box six.

1. Draw an orange line under the block that is not the same.
2. Put a purple X on each block that is the same.

Nice work!

School Daze

Name ______________________

1.

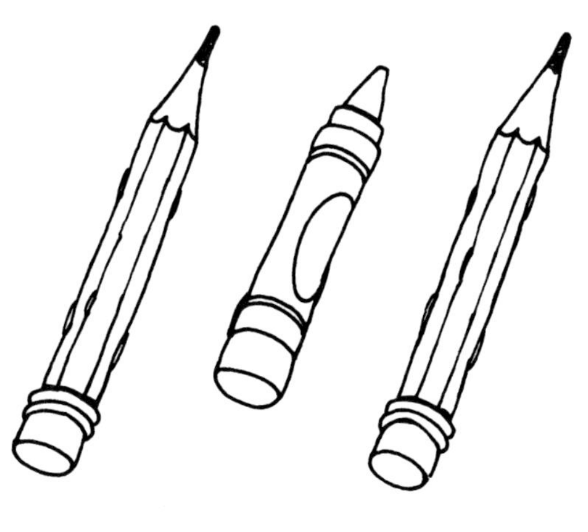

2.

3.

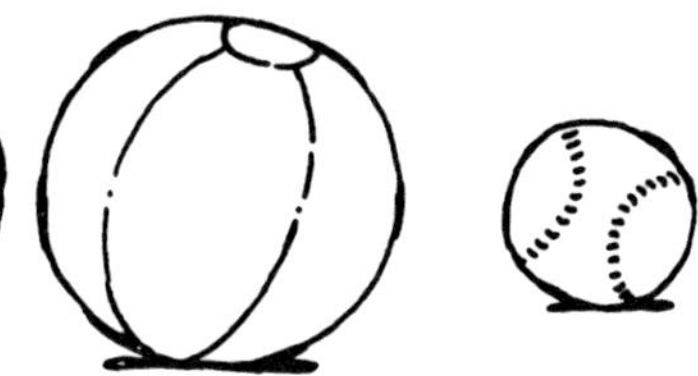

4.

5.

6.

Magic Hat Tricks

Directions: Bring a top hat to class (or any hat you can put picture cards into). Cut apart the pictures on this page and the following two pages. Place all the cards into the hat without letting the children see them. Then, tell the children that you're holding a magic hat and that you're the magician. As you pull a picture out of the hat, they'll be able to see either a part of the picture or the whole thing.

Ask the children to guess what pictures are in the hat as you pull them out. Begin by pulling one of the pictures partway out of the hat. Explain that you're showing a part of the picture. Ask the children to identify the picture. If you need to show more of the picture so the children can identify it, explain that you're still showing a part of the picture. After the children identify the picture, show the whole picture, explaining that now they can see the whole picture.

Let the children take turns being the magician. Be sure to comment whether a child is showing a whole picture or part of a picture. As the children become familiar with the exercise, ask them to tell whether they can see a whole or a part. They may want to experiment by pulling the pictures out from different angles to show different parts.

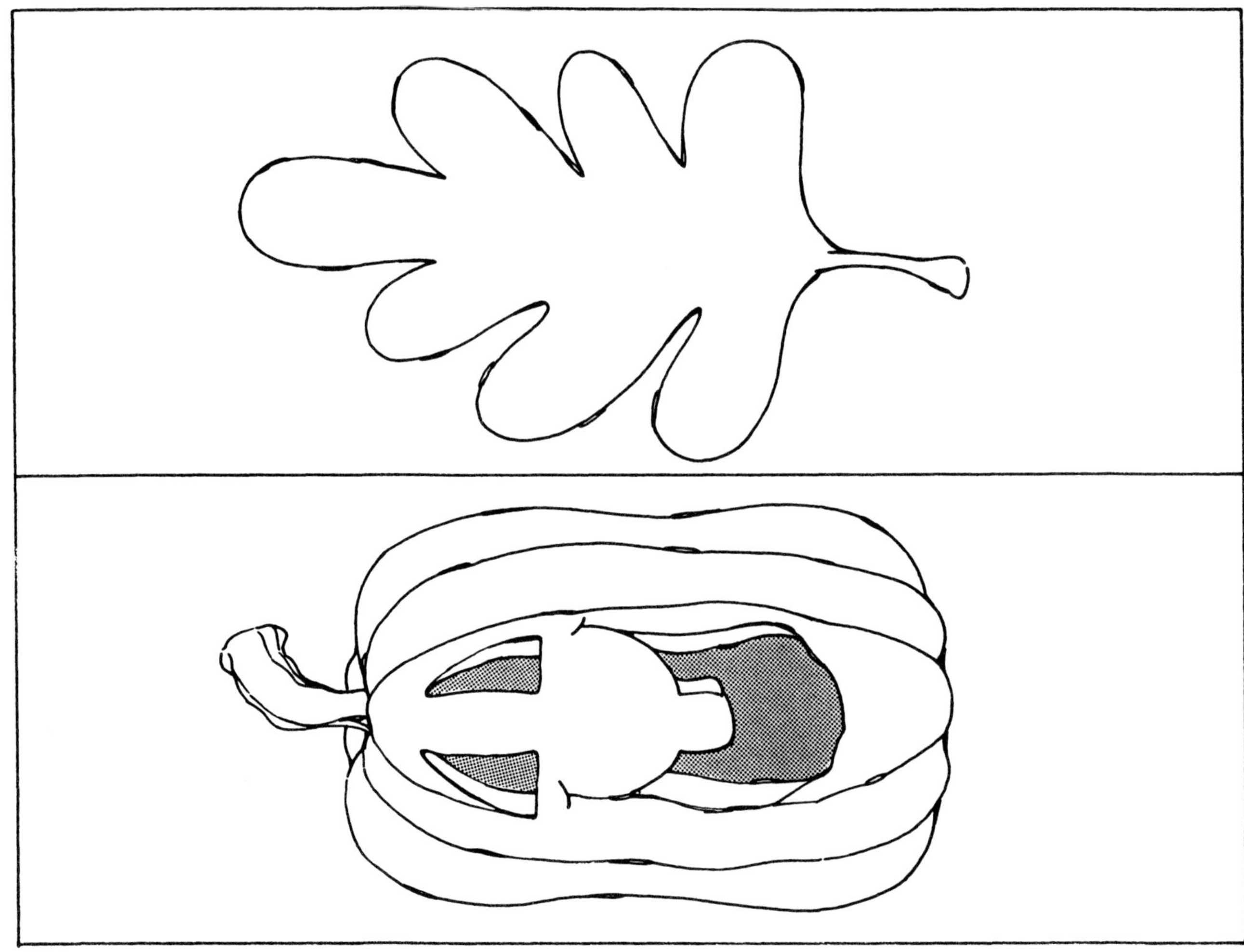

Magic Cards

Name ______________________

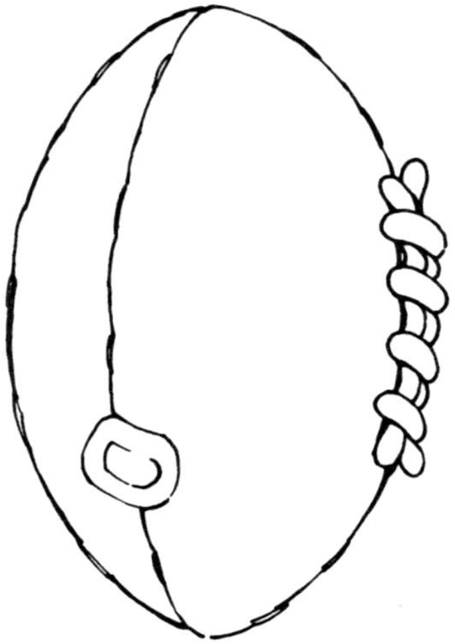

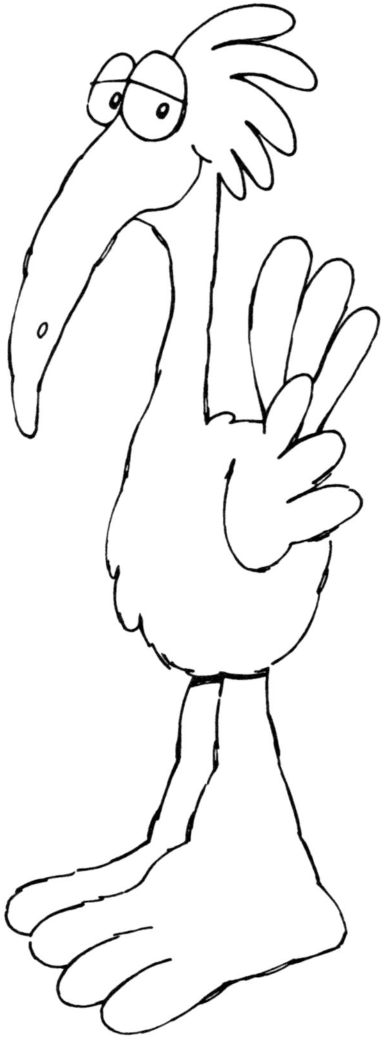

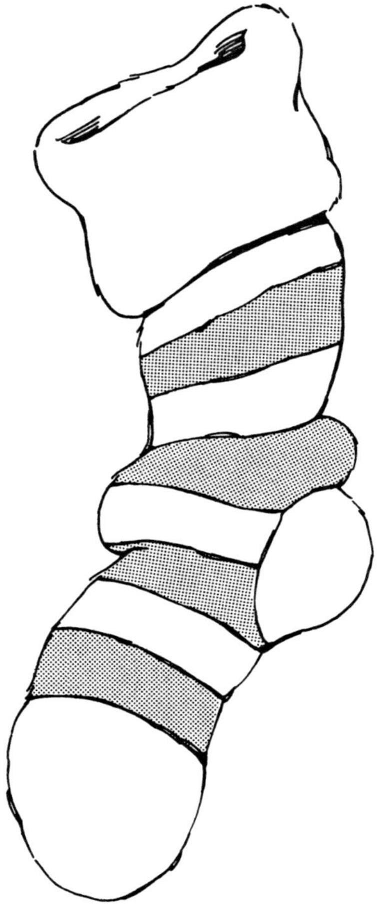

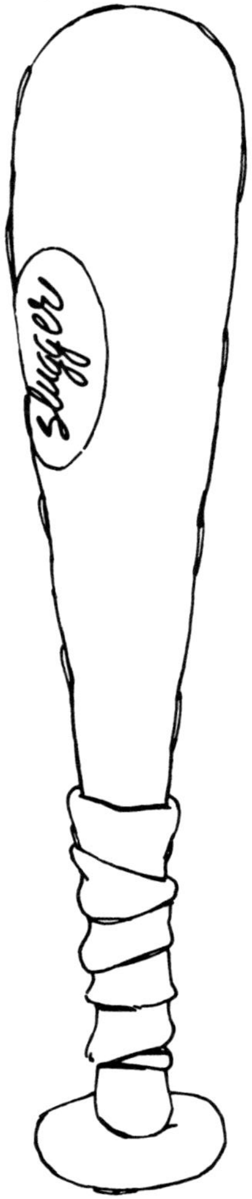

Slugger

Magic Cards, continued

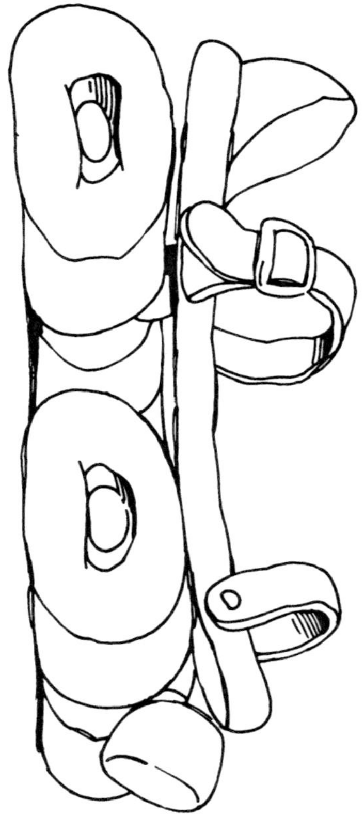

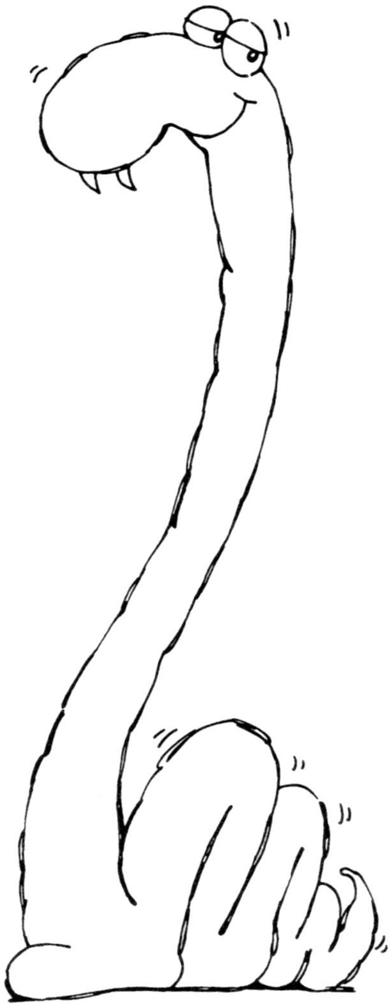

Name ________________________

A
A

Magic Show: Instructions

Give each child a copy of *Magic Show*. Have the children listen carefully and follow your directions. Remind them to listen for the words *whole* and *part*.

1. Put a purple X on the whole rabbit.
2. Draw blue circles around the cards you can only see part of.
3. Color the whole snake red.
4. Color the stars you can only see part of orange.
5. Put blue polka dots on the cape of the whole magician.
6. Color the rabbit you can only see part of brown.
7. Put a green X on the whole bird.
8. Find the tablecloth with circles. Color the circles you can only see part of blue.
9. Color the bird you can only see part of yellow.
10. Color the whole stars green.
11. Find the magician you can only see part of. Draw yellow stripes on his hat.
12. Color the hat of the whole magician black.
13. Draw a yellow square around each whole card.
14. Draw a red line under the roller skate you can only see part of.
15. Color the snake you can only see part of brown.

What a magical picture you've colored!

Magic Show

Name ____________________

Halloween Treats

Directions: Tell the children you're going to read a story about Halloween. Tell them to listen for the words *all*, *some*, and *none* in the story. Each time they hear the word *all*, they should hold up both hands and show all their fingers. Each time they hear the word *some*, they should hold up one hand to show some of their fingers. Each time they hear the word *none*, they should put their hands behind their backs to show none of their fingers. (You may want to have the children practice a few times before you read the story.)

* * * * * * * * * * * * * * * * * * *

It was Halloween and Brennan Bear was going trick-or-treating. All of his friends met at his house so they could go with him. Some of his friends had scary costumes, but none of their costumes was as scary as Brennan's. He was a ghost.

Brennan and his friends walked to all of the houses on Brennan's street. They liked knocking on people's doors and getting treats from them. Some people weren't home, but all the people who were home gave them treats. Some people gave them candy bars and some people gave them small bags of pretzels. Some people gave them little boxes of raisins, but none of the people gave them gum.

When Brennan and his friends got home, all of them looked in their bags to count their treats. None of Brennan's friends were sad because all of them had their favorite treats. Some of his friends were already eating their treats. Yum!

Brennan said, "It's fun getting candy and treats when we go trick-or-treating. I think Halloween is one of the best holidays of the year!"

Questions:

1. Who went trick-or-treating?
2. Tell what Brennan's costume was.
3. Where did Brennan and his friends go trick-or-treating?
4. What treats did Brennan and his friends get?
5. What treat did none of them get?
6. Why were none of Brennan's friends sad?
7. What's another holiday when you get candy or treats?
8. Which is your favorite holiday? Why?
9. If you could dress up in your favorite costume, what would it be?
10. Name some other treats you might get when you go trick-or-treating.

A Haunted House: Instructions

Give each child a copy of *A Haunted House*. Have the children listen carefully and follow your directions. Remind them to listen for the words *all*, *some*, and *none*.

1. Give some of the bears green shirts.
2. Color all of the moon yellow.
3. Color all the bears' shoes black.
4. Give some of the bears red pants.
5. Color the bears' ears, but make sure none of the them are blue.
6. Give some of the bats black ears.
7. Give all the bats brown wings.
8. Give some of the bears yellow trick or treat bags.
9. Give each bear a hat, but make sure none of the bears have green hats.
10. Color all the bears' heads brown.
11. Add stripes on some of the bears' shirts.
12. Add brown polka dots on some of the bears' pants.
13. Color all the cobwebs black.
14. Give some of the bats brown ears.
15. Color some of the bears' paws brown and none of them black.

All your bears look great!

A Haunted House

Name ____________________

Halloween Hunt

Directions: Draw the map on the following page on a chalkboard. Name all the objects so your children know what they are. Then, read the story below. As you read the story, have the children help you decide where to draw the path. Encourage the children to listen carefully, especially for the words *through* and *around*.

* * * * * * * * * * * * * * * * * * *

Brennan has a big field next to his house. He and his friends love to climb the trees, run through the tall grass, fish in the long, curvy river, run around the fences, and catch frogs in the small pond. But they never play in the dark caves! (Point to the objects on the chalkboard as you talk about them.)

One Halloween, Brennan's mom hid a surprise in the field. Then, she gave Brennan a map for a Halloween Hunt. Listen to the clues on the map. Let's see if we can find the surprise Brennan's mom hid in the field. Help me draw the path where Brennan should go.

1. Start at the X beside the tree. You can't go through the tree, so go around it.
2. The river is too deep to go through, so go around it. Make sure you stay away from the dark caves and go through the tall grass.
3. Go to the other tree. Can you go through a tree? No! Go around it.
4. Go to Mr. Brown's fence. If you went through the fence, you might break a board. You had better go around the fence!
5. Wade through the top of the small frog pond. Are your tennis shoes squishing yet?
6. Go to Mr. Miller's fence and go around it.
7. Go back to the X.
8. Now, look at what we drew. What was the Halloween surprise?

Questions:

1. Tell what Brennan has next to his house.
2. What do Brennan and his friends like to do in the long, curvy river?
3. Where is a place Brennan and his friends never play?
4. Tell what Brennan's mom gave him to help him find his surprise.
5. Name something the map told Brennan to do.
6. How did Brennan get to the other side of the small frog pond?
7. What was Brennan's surprise?
8. Name some other things that could be in a field.
9. Why do you think Brennan and his friends never played in the caves?
10. Do you like to follow maps? Why or why not?

Halloween Hunt, continued

Directions: Draw this map on a chalkboard without the dotted lines. Then, follow the directions on the previous page. As you read the story, have the children help you decide where to draw the path. (The dotted lines show the key to the Halloween Hunt.)

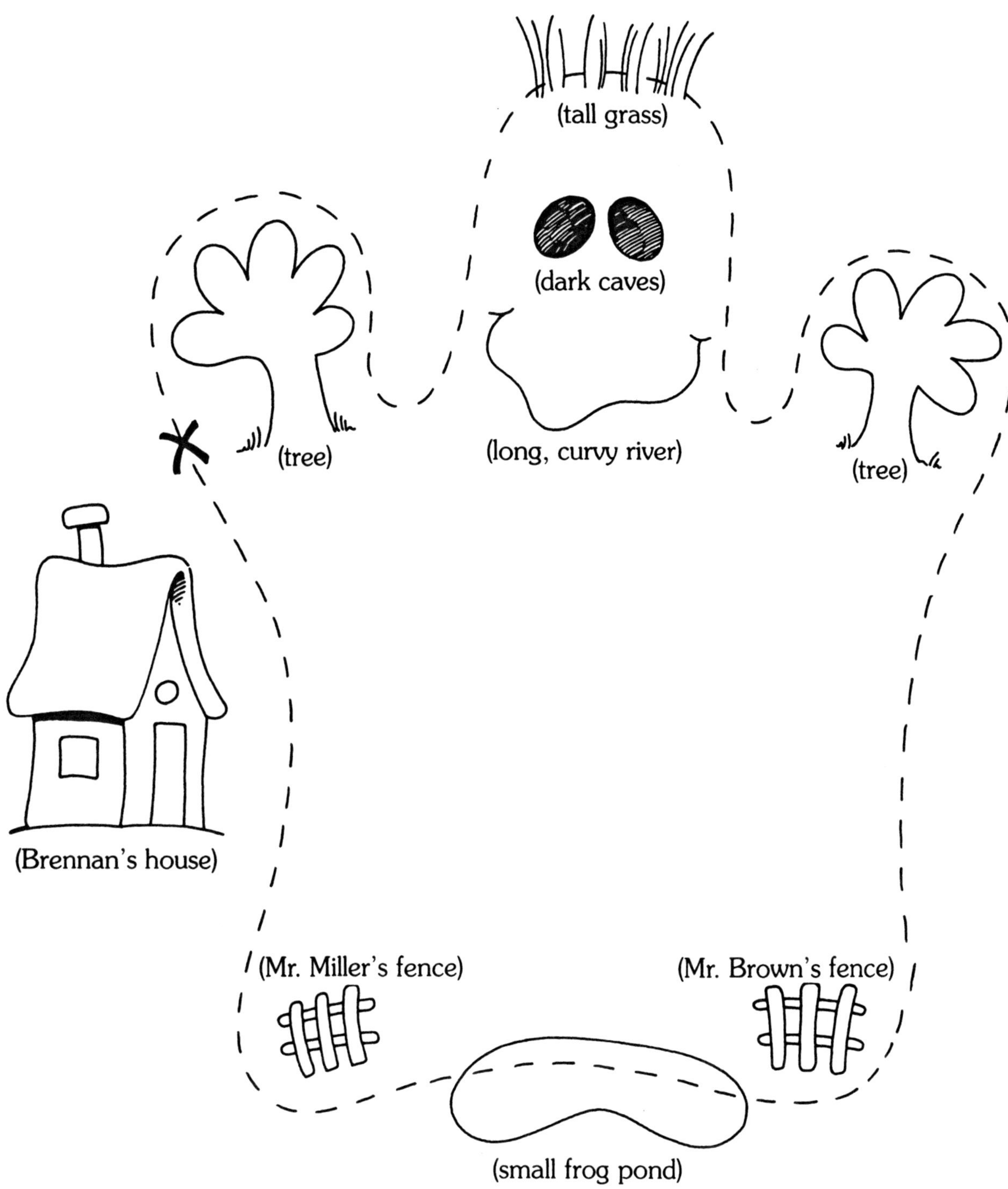

Wanda Witch: Instructions

Give each child a copy of *Wanda Witch*. Have the children listen carefully and follow your directions. Remind them to listen for the words *through* and *around*.

1. Draw a red line through the happy jack-o'-lantern.
2. Draw a green collar around the cat's neck. Now, color the cat black.
3. Draw an orange circle around the cat's paws.
4. Draw a red arrow through the moon.
5. Draw a purple square around the pumpkin that doesn't have a face.
6. Draw a yellow line through the witch's hat.
7. Draw an orange line through one of the bat's wings.
8. Draw a yellow circle around the moon.
9. Draw a green line through both of the witch's shoes.
10. Draw blue circles around both jack-o'-lanterns' eyes.
11. Draw a black arrow through the pumpkin that doesn't have a face.
12. Draw a blue square around one of the witch's ears.
13. Draw a green circle around one of the bats.
14. Draw a purple line through one of the witch's hands.
15. Draw a black square around the sad jack-o'-lantern.

Halloween is just around the corner!

Wanda Witch

Name ______________________________

A Halloween Picture

Directions: Use the pictures on the following three pages as you tell the story below. Be sure to point to the objects as you describe their position on the page.

✸ ✸ ✸ ✸ ✸ ✸ ✸ ✸ ✸ ✸ ✸ ✸ ✸ ✸ ✸ ✸ ✸ ✸ ✸

Brennan Bear decided to draw a Halloween picture. He got some paper and crayons. He drew a picture. This is what it looked like. (Hold up *Brennan's First Picture.*) He was so proud of his picture that he took it to show it to his mom. When she saw the picture, she said, "Brennan, you drew a very nice picture, but it isn't a Halloween picture. You drew Santa Claus at the top of your paper, a Christmas tree in the middle, and a present at the bottom. That's a Christmas picture. You'd better try again!"

So, Brennan got some more paper and drew another picture. This is what it looked like. (Hold up *Brennan's Second Picture.*) When he showed the picture to his mom, she said, "Oh no, Brennan. You did it again! You drew a Pilgrim at the top of your paper, a turkey in the middle, and an Indian at the bottom. That's not a Halloween picture. That's a Thanksgiving picture. Try one more time to draw a Halloween picture."

So, Brennan got some more paper and drew another picture. This time he was sure he had drawn a Halloween picture. This is what his picture looked like. (Hold up *Brennan's Third Picture.*) Again, he showed the picture to his mom. This time, she said, "That's much better, Brennan. This time you drew a jack-o'-lantern at the top of your paper, a bat in the middle, and a ghost at the bottom. You drew a very nice Halloween picture. I'm glad you figured out what things go with Halloween!"

Questions:

1. What did Brennan draw at the top of the Christmas picture?
2. What did Brennan draw in the middle of the Christmas picture?
3. What did Brennan draw at the bottom of the Christmas picture?
4. What did Brennan draw in the middle of the Thanksgiving picture?
5. What did Brennan draw at the bottom of the Thanksgiving picture?
6. What did Brennan draw at the top of the Thanksgiving picture
7. What did Brennan draw at the bottom of the Halloween picture?
8. What did Brennan draw at the top of the Halloween picture
9. What did Brennan draw in the middle of the Halloween picture?
10. Describe what you like best about Halloween.

Note: Feel free to show the pictures to the children to help remind them what pictures Brennan drew on each page.

Brennan's First Picture

Brennan's Second Picture

Brennan's Third Picture

Halloween Haunters: Instructions

Give each child copies of the *Halloween Haunters* pages. Have the children listen carefully and follow your directions. Remind them to listen for the words *top*, *middle*, and *bottom*.

Look at the jack-o'-lanterns.

1. Put a green X on the top jack-o'-lantern.
2. Put a blue circle around the bottom jack-o'-lantern.
3. Color the middle jack-o'-lantern orange.

Look at the ghosts.

1. Draw a purple tie on the bottom ghost.
2. Draw a black line on the middle ghost.
3. Draw a red hat on the top ghost.

Look at the bats.

1. Draw a green square around the middle bat.
2. Color the bottom bat brown.
3. Draw a blue circle around the top bat.

Look at the scarecrows.

1. Color the hat on the middle scarecrow brown.
2. Draw a green trick or treat bag on the arm of the top scarecrow.
3. Color the coat on the bottom scarecrow red.

Look at the cats.

1. Put a yellow circle around the bottom cat.
2. Color the cat in the middle black.
3. Draw a purple line under the top cat.

Look at the empty boxes.

1. Draw a scary face in the bottom box.
2. Draw a broom in the top box.
3. Draw a red apple in the middle box.

Happy Haunting!

Halloween Haunters

Name ____________________

Halloween Haunters, continued

Name ______________________

Home Lesson

Dear ________________,

During the month of October, we have been working on these concepts: *same, not the same, whole, part, all, some, none, through, around, top, middle,* and *bottom*. You can help your child review these concepts by giving your child the sheet attached to this page. Read the directions below and encourage your child to listen carefully and follow your directions. Here are the materials you will need: a box of eight crayons, a table, a chair, and a quiet place to work.

Directions:

1. Draw three orange jack-o'-lanterns on top of the fence. Make two happy and one sad.
2. Draw a green line through the witch's broom.
3. Add some stars at the bottom of the witch's clothes.
4. Color the cloud you can see part of blue.
5. Color all the stones you can see on the roof yellow.
6. Draw a black circle around the witch's feet.
7. Color some of the fence boards brown and some of them yellow.
8. Put a purple X at the top of the witch's hat.
9. Use a blue crayon to circle the jack-o'-lanterns with the same faces.
10. Put a blue X on the jack-o'-lantern that doesn't have the same face.
11. Draw four red apples at the bottom of the fence. Make sure that none of them has leaves.
12. Draw an orange star in the middle of the witch's hat.
13. Color all the witch's fingers yellow.
14. Add brown spots to the stones that look the same.
15. Color the whole cloud black.

Have a safe Halloween!

Sincerely,

____

Name ______________________

A Walk in the Woods

Directions: Tell the children you're going to read a story. Ask them to listen for the words *under* and *over*. Each time they hear you say the word *under*, they should put their hands under their chins. Each time they hear you say *over*, they should put their hands over their heads.

* * * * * * * * * * * * * * * * * * *

It was a sunny fall day, so Brennan decided to take a walk in the woods near his home. As he walked through the woods, he saw many things. First, he saw a rabbit hopping over some bushes. The rabbit sure moved quickly!

Next, he saw a worm crawl under a rock. The worm sure moved slowly! Brennan thought it would take the worm forever to disappear under the rock.

Next, Brennan saw a beautiful deer jump over a tree that had fallen down. Brennan ran and jumped over the tree, too. That was fun!

Brennan also saw a squirrel sitting under an oak tree. It was eating acorns. Brennan walked closer to the squirrel, but as soon as the squirrel saw him, he scampered up into the tree.

As Brennan walked further into the woods, he climbed over big rocks and tree stumps. He walked under the low branches of some big trees, looking up at the pretty fall leaves.

Soon, Brennan came to a stream in the woods. The cool water splashed over the rocks as it went downstream. There was a bridge that went over the stream, but Brennan decided not to use the bridge — he wanted to jump over the stream. First, he backed up a little ways. Then, he ran toward the stream and jumped as far as he could. Splash! Oh, no! Brennan didn't quite make it over the stream. He landed in the stream. Brrr!

"Next time, I'll use the bridge to get over the stream," thought Brennan. "I'd probably stay a lot drier!"

Questions:

1. What time of the year was it?
2. Name some animals Brennan saw.
3. Which animals hopped or jumped over things? What did they jump over?
4. What did the squirrel do when it saw Brennan coming?
5. What did Brennan climb over?
6. Why didn't Brennan use the bridge?
7. Tell what a stream looks like.
8. Why would Brennan stay drier if he walked on the bridge?
9. Where's another place you can go to climb over and under lots of things?
10. If you could be a forest animal, which animal would you be? Why?

Fall Fun: Instructions

Give each child a copy of *Fall Fun*. Have the children listen carefully and follow your directions. Remind them to listen for the words *under* and *over*.

Look at row one.

1. Draw a yellow bee over the flower.
2. Draw a brown worm under the tree.
3. Put a red X under the pumpkin.
4. Draw a purple bug under the flower.
5. Draw a blue bird over the tree.
6. Draw a black line over the pumpkin.

Look at row two.

1. Draw a red line over the turkey.
2. Draw a black fork over the corn.
3. Draw a purple fish under the ship.
4. Draw a brown line under the turkey.
5. Draw a blue plate under the corn.
6. Draw an orange sun over the ship.

Look at row three.

1. Draw a Pilgrim face under the hat.
2. Draw a yellow plate under the pie.
3. Put a green X over the tepee.
4. Draw a red line over the hat.
5. Put a blue X over the pie.
6. Draw a brown bird under the tepee.

Look at row four.

1. Draw a red mouth over the drumstick.
2. Draw an Indian's head under the headdress.
3. Draw a brown stick over the apple.
4. Draw a blue line under the drumstick.
5. Draw a purple line over the headdress.
6. Draw a brown worm under the apple.

What fun for the fall!

Fall Fun

Name ______________________

1.   

2.   

3.   

4. 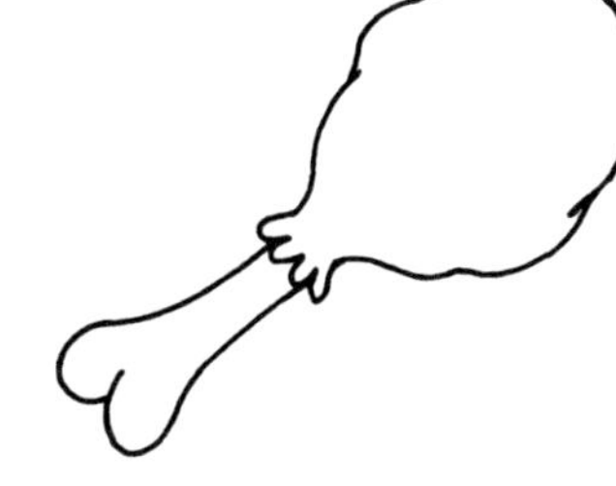  

Thomas Turkey: Instructions

Demonstrate the meaning of the words *beside* and *between* by having the children stand side by side at the front of the classroom. Ask the children to tell you which child is beside a given child and which child is between two children.

When the children understand the concepts, give each child a copy of *Thomas Turkey*. Enlarge one copy of the picture and hang it in the front of the classroom. Introduce the turkey as Thomas Turkey, a friend of Brennan's. Explain that Thomas needs help getting ready for Thanksgiving. Color the feathers as they are labeled, and have the children do the same. Then, explain that part of Thomas's tail feathers are ready for Thanksgiving — the ones that you have colored. But, he needs the rest of his feathers colored, too. Encourage the children to listen carefully and follow your directions. Remind them to listen for the words *beside* and *between*.

1. Color the feather between the blue feathers brown.
2. Color the feather beside the red feather orange.
3. Color the feather between the yellow feathers green.
4. Color the feather between the yellow feather and the blue feather orange.
5. Color the feather beside the purple feather red.
6. Color the feather between the blue feather and the red feather yellow.

What a colorful turkey!

Thomas Turkey

Name ______________________

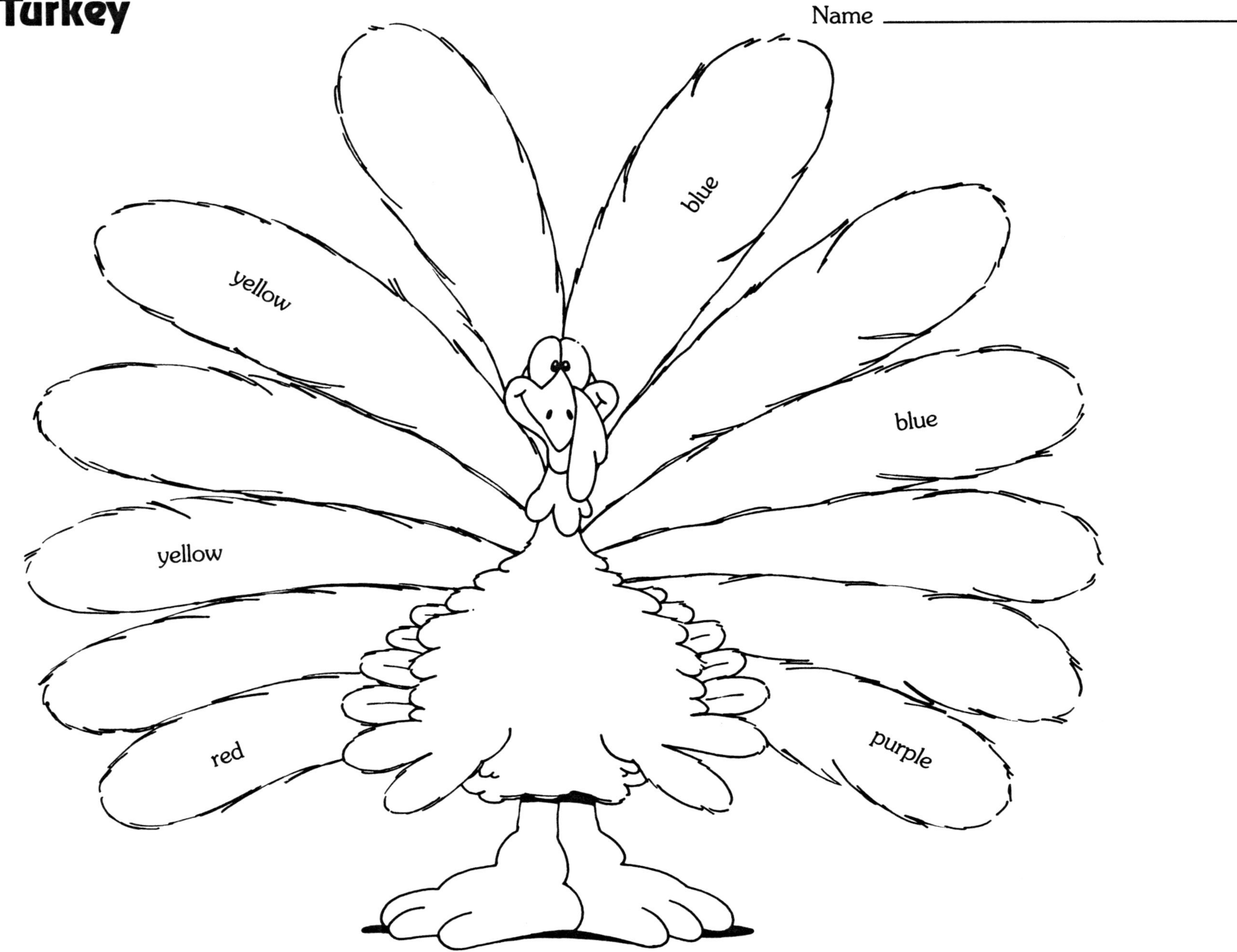

Thanksgiving Row: Instructions

Give each child a copy of *Thanksgiving Row*. Have the children listen carefully and follow your directions. Remind them to listen for the words *beside* and *between*.

1. Find the turkey between two Pilgrims. Color that turkey's tail feathers orange.
2. Find the turkey beside the Indian. Color that turkey's tail feathers red and yellow.
3. Find the turkey between a Pilgrim and the Indian. Draw a red apple beside that turkey.
4. Find the Pilgrim between two turkeys. Color that Pilgrim's suit blue.
5. Find the Pilgrim beside the turkey with an apple. Draw an orange pumpkin beside that Pilgrim.
6. Find the Pilgrim that isn't beside the turkey with red and yellow feathers. Color that Pilgrim's hat brown.
7. Find the turkey between two Pilgrims. Draw a piece of yellow corn beside the turkey's feet.
8. Use a brown crayon to color the turkey's body that's between the Pilgrim and the Indian.
9. Find the Indian. Color the feather in his headdress that's between two other feathers.
10. Find the Pilgrim between two turkeys. Color that Pilgrim's hat black.
11. Find the Pilgrim that isn't beside a turkey with an apple. Color that Pilgrim's suit brown.
12. Find the turkey between two Pilgrims. Color that turkey's body yellow.
13. Draw a red line under the turkey that isn't beside the Indian.
14. Find the Pilgrim between two turkeys. Color that Pilgrim's shoes blue.
15. Find the turkey beside the Indian. Draw a yellow sun over that turkey.

Who would you like to stand between?

Thanksgiving Row

Name ______________________

November: *beside, between*

Honey

Directions: Give a copy of the following page to each child. Then, encourage the children to listen carefully as you read the story below. After you read the story, ask the children the questions listed at the bottom of the page and let the children color their worksheets.

* * * * * * * * * * * * * * * * * * *

Brennan was very excited. It was Thanksgiving Day and he loved to eat turkey. His mom was busy in the kitchen, so Brennan decided to help by setting the table. He carefully set out the glasses, dishes, silverware, and napkins. There, the table looked perfect for a Thanksgiving dinner!

Then, his mom said, "Brennan, I'm very busy fixing the potatoes for our dinner. Could you get some honey from the beehives? We need it for our biscuits."

"Okay," said Brennan. "I love honey!"

Brennan quickly got a large bowl for the honey and skipped out the door. He hurried to the back of the field where his family had three beehives. All of the beehives had bees buzzing around them. (Hold up *Bees and Honey*.) The first beehive had the fewest bees buzzing around it. It only had two bees. The next beehive had a few more bees buzzing around it. It had five bees. The last beehive had the most bees. It had ten!

"Well," thought Brennan, "I'm not going to reach into the last beehive. I would probably get stung because that beehive has the most bees around it. I'll get some honey from the first beehive. It has the fewest bees, so I'll have a better chance of getting the honey safely."

Brennan waited until the two bees were looking the other way. Then, he reached into the beehive and pulled out some honey. "Whew!" thought Brennan. "I'm glad I didn't get stung. This honey looks delicious!"

Brennan took the honey into the house and set it in the middle of the table. Brennan's mom said, "Thank you for getting the honey. This is going to be a delicious Thanksgiving dinner!"

Questions:

1. What holiday is it?
2. Why did Brennan's mom want honey?
3. Tell how many beehives Brennan's family has.
4. Which beehive had the most bees?
5. Why did Brennan get honey from the first beehive?
6. Tell where Brennan put the honey when he brought it inside.
7. What else could you put honey on?
8. Describe your favorite Thanksgiving food.
9. Where would you get honey if you didn't have a beehive?
10. Pretend you're a bee. What would you think if Brennan took your honey?

Bees and Honey

Name ______________________

November: *most, fewest*

Indian Feathers: Instructions

Give each child a copy of *Indian Feathers*. Have the children listen carefully and follow your directions. Remind them to listen for the words *most* and *fewest*.

1. Find the bear with the fewest feathers. Color the bear's mouth red.
2. Find the bear with the most arrows. Draw another arrow in the bear's paw.
3. Find the bear with the fewest necklaces. Put brown moccasins on the bear's feet.
4. Find the bear with the most dots on his clothing. Color his clothing blue.
5. Find the bear with the fewest arrows. Draw a yellow sun above that bear.
6. Find the bear with the fewest feathers. Draw a black rain cloud above that bear.
7. Find the bear with the most arrows. Color those arrows red.
8. Find the bear with the fewest necklaces. Color that bear's necklace yellow.
9. Find the bear with the fewest arrows. Color that bear's arrow orange.
10. Find the bear with the most feathers. Draw green grass under that bear.
11. Find the bear with the most arrows. Color that bear's feathers orange.
12. Find the bear with the fewest feathers. Color that bear's feathers blue.
13. Find the bear with the most necklaces. Color two necklaces purple and one necklace red.
14. Find the bear with the most feathers. Color that bear's feathers red.
15. Find the bear with the fewest dots on his clothing. Color that bear's clothing green.

What pretty Indian feathers you colored!

Indian Feathers

Name ______________________

November: *most, fewest*

Thanksgiving Feast

Directions: Cut out the pictures on the following two pages. As you read the story below, have the children help you "feed" the foods to Brennan as you talk about them. You may need to help the children cut the pictures in half if they have to feed Brennan half of the food.

* * * * * * * * * * * * * * * * * * *

Brennan patted his stomach. "I'm getting fat," he thought. "I'd better not eat too much for Thanksgiving dinner." He sat down at the table and his mouth began to water as he looked down at his favorite foods. First, he picked up a turkey leg. "I'll only eat half," he said. "Yum, yum! I love turkey," said Brennan. "I'll just eat a little bit more." Gobble, gobble. He ate the whole thing!

"Oh, well," thought Brennan, "I'll only eat half of my mashed potatoes." He took one spoonful, then another, until he had eaten half of his mashed potatoes. "Yum! I love mashed potatoes even more than turkey. I'll just take one more little bite," said Brennan. Gobble, gobble. He ate the whole thing!

"Oh, well," thought Brennan, "I'll only eat half of my stuffing." He began to eat his stuffing. He only ate half, but it tasted so good! "I love stuffing even more than turkey and potatoes," said Brennan. He took one more little, teeny bite, and then....gobble, gobble. He ate the whole thing!

"Oh, well," thought Brennan, "I'll only eat half of my cranberries." He ate one spoonful, then another. "Yum! I love cranberries even more than stuffing, potatoes, and turkey," said Brennan. "I'll just take one more little, teeny, tiny bite." Gobble, gobble. Yes, he ate the whole thing!

Brennan's mom brought out the pumpkin pie. "Well, I love pumpkin pie even more than cranberries, stuffing, potatoes, and turkey," said Brennan. "I know I can't eat just half!" So, he ate the whole thing! "Grumble, growl," went Brennan's stomach. Oh, Brennan had a stomachache!

"Do you want half of a stomach tablet?" asked his mom.

"No," said Brennan, "I need the whole thing!"

Questions:

1. Why did Brennan only want to eat half of everything?
2. Why did Brennan always end up eating the whole thing?
3. What did Brennan eat for Thanksgiving dinner?
4. Tell what food Brennan liked the best.
5. How much of the pumpkin pie did Brennan eat?
6. Why did Brennan have a stomachache?
7. Name some other desserts besides pumpkin pie.
8. What do you do when you feel full?
9. What do you call something if it tastes good?
10. What is something you would only want to eat half of? Explain your answer.

Food for the Feast

Directions: Cut out the pictures below. As you read *Thanksgiving Feast*, have the children help you "feed" the foods to Brennan as you talk about them. You may need to help the children cut the pictures in half if they have to feed Brennan half of the food.

Feed Me!

Directions: Cut out Brennan's mouth on the dotted lines. As you read *Thanksgiving Feast*, have the children help you "feed" the foods through Brennan's mouth as you talk about them.

Thanksgiving Day: Instructions

Give each child a copy of *Thanksgiving Day*. Have the children listen carefully and follow your directions. Remind them to listen for the words *half* and *whole*.

Look at box one.

1. Put a red X on the turkey you can only see half of.
2. Color the turkey that's whole brown.

Look at box two.

1. Color the whole glass of milk brown.
2. Color the half glass of milk white.

Look at box three.

1. Circle the half ears of corn with your purple crayon.
2. Color the whole ears of corn green and yellow.

Look at box four.

1. Draw an orange line through the potato you can see half of.
2. Color the potato that's whole brown.

Look at box five.

1. Color the pie that's whole orange.
2. Color the half pie blue.

Look at box six.

1. Color the whole sail of one ship red.
2. Color half of the sail on the other ship blue.

Look at box seven.

1. Color the half tepee black.
2. Color the whole tepee green.

Look at box eight.

1. Draw a blue circle around the hat that's whole.
2. Use your black crayon to finish the half hat to make it whole.

Are you ready for Thanksgiving Day?

Thanksgiving Day

Name ______________________

1.

2.

3.

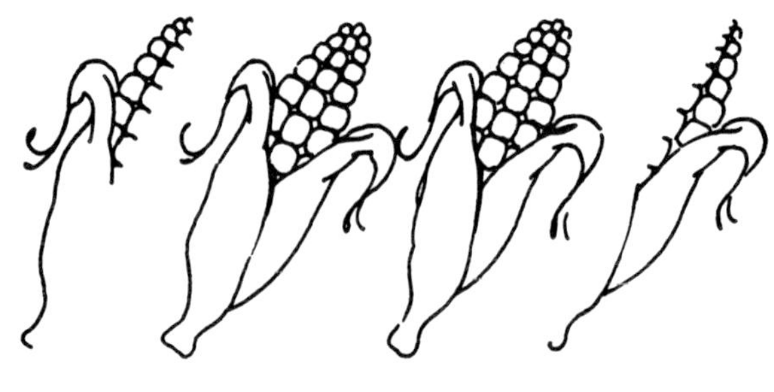

4.

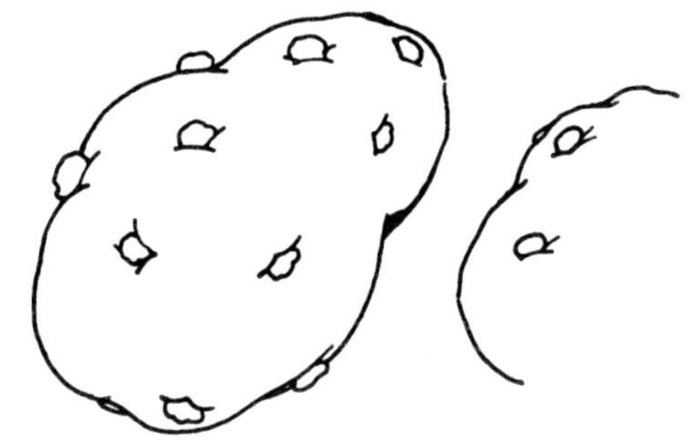

5.

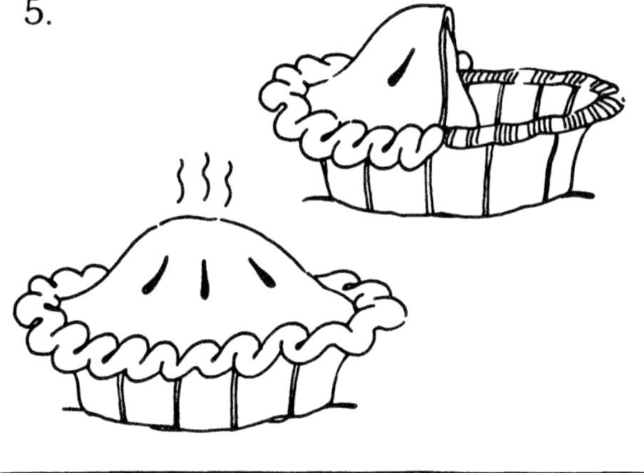

6.

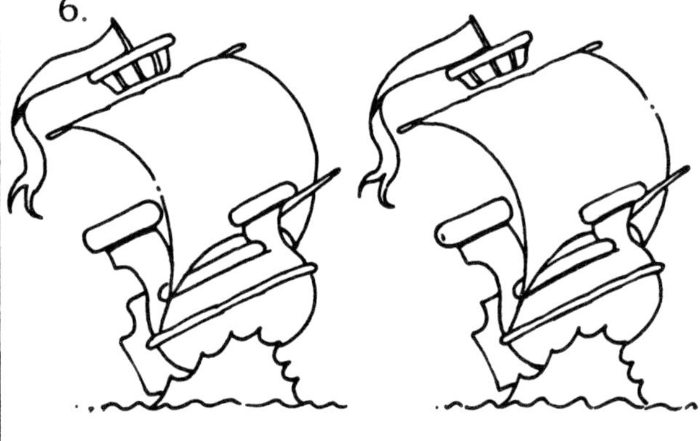

7.

8.

Home Lesson

Dear ________________,

During the month of November, we have been working on these concepts: *over, under, beside, between, most, fewest, half,* and *whole*. You can help your child review these concepts by giving your child the sheet attached to this page. Read the directions below and encourage your child to listen carefully and follow your directions. Here are the materials you will need: a box of eight crayons, a table, a chair, and a quiet place to work.

Directions:

Look at row one.

1. Put a green X under the pie.
2. Draw a yellow curvy line between the socks.
3. Color the shirt with the fewest stripes brown.

Look at row two.

1. Draw an orange star over the little bunny.
2. Draw a blue line under the glass with the most milk.
3. Draw a green square around the spoon that's whole.

Look at row three.

1. Draw a purple line over the Indian with the most feathers.
2. Put a brown X beside the sad clown.
3. Draw a black curvy line between the turkeys.

Look at row four.

1. Color half of the apple red.
2. Color the caterpillar with the fewest legs yellow.
3. Draw a green smiley face beside the happy cat.

Have a Happy Thanksgiving!

Sincerely,

____

Name ____________________

1.

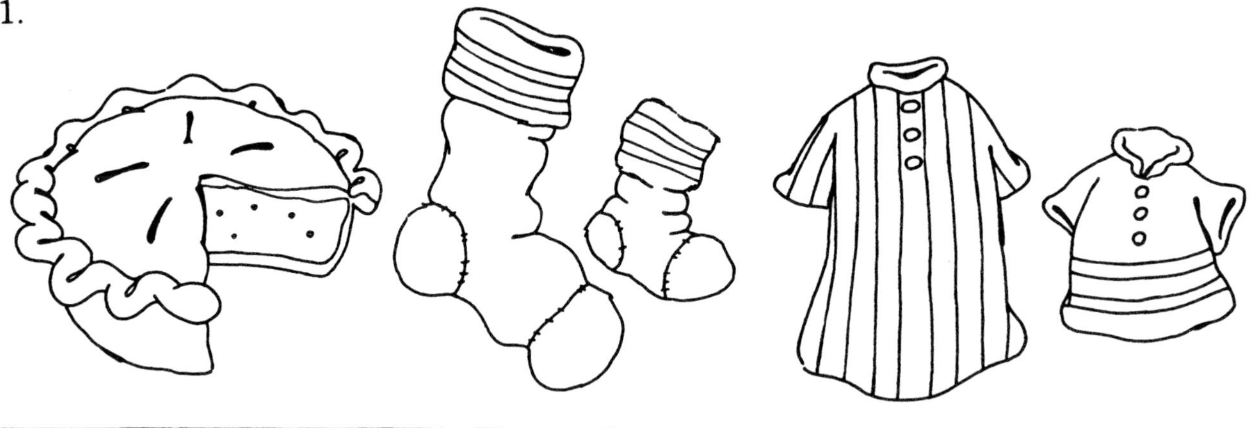

2.

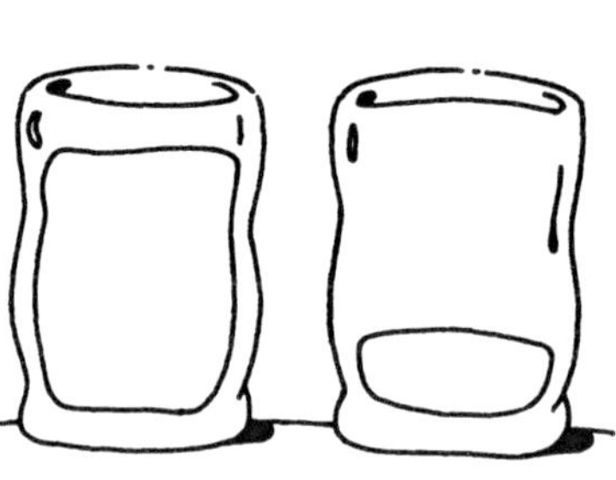

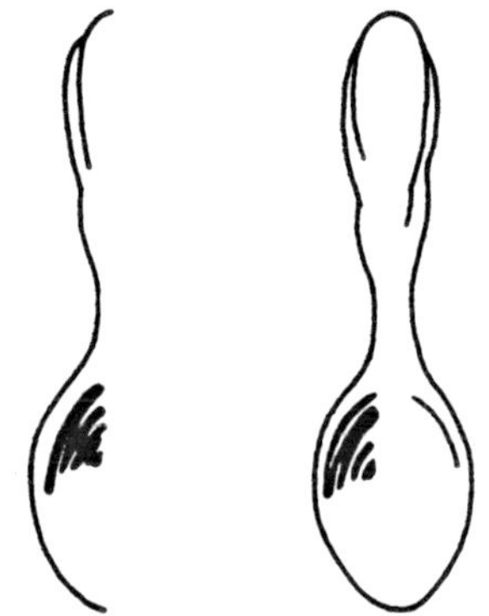

3.

4.

Fall Concept Check

Directions: Use this concept check to see how well your children remember the concepts they've learned in the last few months. Give each child the following page. Then, have the children listen carefully and follow your directions.

1. Color the thing you always use to rake leaves brown.
2. Circle the bird that's out of the nest with a red crayon.
3. Draw two more leaves on the tree with the fewest leaves. Make sure the leaves are not the same color.
4. Color the cloud you can only see part of blue.
5. Color the pumpkin beside the haystack orange.
6. Draw a brown bat flying over the sun.
7. Give some of the pumpkins green stems.
8. Draw a purple line through one pumpkin.
9. Put a purple X on something that's never made of wood.
10. Color the trunk of the tree away from the bear brown.
11. Color the bird in the nest blue.
12. Color two leaves on the big tree the same color.
13. Color the cloud that's whole black.
14. Draw a yellow circle around the tree with the most leaves.
15. Draw an orange pumpkin next to the big tree.
16. Draw a red line under the sun.
17. Color half of the sun yellow.
18. Draw a red apple between the pumpkins at the bottom of the page.
19. Color all the leaves in the pile orange.
20. Color the leaves on the small tree. Make sure none of the leaves are green.
21. Put a red X in the middle of one pumpkin.
22. Draw a green hat on top of the bear's head.
23. Put a yellow X on the bird that's leaning backward.

You sure have learned a lot this fall!

Name ______________________

Recess Fun

Directions: Have the children stand beside their desks. Tell them to listen for the words *behind* and *in front of* in the story you are going to read. Each time they hear you say the word *behind*, they should stand behind their desks. Each time they hear you say *in front of*, they should stand in front of their desks.

❄ ❄ ❄ ❄ ❄ ❄ ❄ ❄ ❄ ❄ ❄ ❄ ❄ ❄ ❄ ❄ ❄ ❄ ❄

Brennan heard the bell ring. "Yay!" he thought. "It's recess time." He put on his winter coat and got in line behind his friend Bernie. Brennan's teacher said, "Brennan, please come up here and stand in front of the line. You've worked very hard in class today, so I want you to be our leader." "Thank you," said Brennan as he walked to the head of the line.

Brennan led his class quietly down the hall. When they got to the door, Brennan stood behind it to hold it open for everyone in his class as they went outside.

Brennan and his classmates had fun at recess. First, they played tag so they would stay warm. Brennan raced in front of the slide just in time to tag Bernie. "You're it!" he exclaimed.

After they played tag, Brennan and some of his classmates played hide-and-seek. Brennan hid behind a big oak tree, but someone found him.

After the hide-and-seek game, Brennan and his friends played follow the leader. Everyone stood in a line, with Brennan in front of everyone else. Everyone in the line had to copy what Brennan did. He sure had fun being the leader!

The last thing Brennan did at recess was to push Bernie on the swing. He had to stand behind Bernie so he could give him a big push. Just as he finished pushing Bernie, the bell rang again. "Gosh," said Brennan, "it's time to go inside already." He got in front of the line and led his class back to the room. "Recess is a lot of fun," thought Brennan. "I wish it would last all day!"

Questions:

1. Where is Brennan?
2. Tell why the teacher picked Brennan to be the leader.
3. What did Brennan do at recess?
4. Where did Brennan stand when he pushed Bernie on the swing?
5. What could Brennan wear outside besides his winter coat?
6. Why was it important for everyone to be quiet as they walked down the hall?
7. What are some things you like to do at recess?
8. Tell how to play hide-and-seek.
9. Why do you think Brennan wants recess to last all day?
10. Would you like recess to last all day? Explain your answer.

On the Playground: Instructions

Give each child a copy of *On the Playground*. Have the children listen carefully and follow your directions. Remind them to listen for the words *behind* and *in front of*.

1. Color the cloud in front of the sun blue.
2. Color the bear behind the tree brown.
3. Draw an orange basketball by the bear in front of the slide.
4. Find the bear standing behind a swing. Give him a red hat.
5. Look at the bears playing follow the leader. Give the bear in front of the girl bear a purple coat.
6. Give the bear in front of the tree green boots.
7. Draw a yellow hat on the bear in front of the swing.
8. Find the bear behind the girl bear. Color his boots black.
9. Put two blue buttons on the coat of the bear behind the swing.
10. Look at the three bears playing follow the leader. Circle the bear behind the leader with a red crayon.
11. Draw a brown football by the bear in front of the tree.
12. Draw a purple bird in front of one of the clouds.
13. Put a green X on the bear in front of the slide.
14. Give the bear in front of the swing a black coat.
15. Find the bear behind the girl bear. Color his coat blue.

What a fun day on the playground!

On the Playground

Name ______________________

28

1

December: *behind, in front of*

Brennan's Smallest Friend

Directions: Use the pictures on the following five pages as you tell the story below. Be sure to point to the objects as you describe their size.

❄ ❄ ❄ ❄ ❄ ❄ ❄ ❄ ❄ ❄ ❄ ❄ ❄ ❄ ❄ ❄ ❄ ❄ ❄

Brennan has many friends. (Show *Brennan's Friends*.) His friends are all different sizes. Rodney Rabbit is a small friend. Chuck Chipmunk is even smaller. But Max Mouse is the smallest of Brennan's friends.

One day, Brennan went to visit Max Mouse. Max had red spots all over his face and he looked very sad. Brennan asked, "What's wrong, Max?" "Oh, Brennan! I have the chicken pox and I can't leave my mouse hole for a whole week. And, Christmas is almost here! Since I can't leave, I can't get a Christmas tree. I'm so sad!"

Brennan replied, "Don't worry, Max. I'll get a tree for you." So, Brennan left to find the perfect tree for Max. First, he looked at three trees. (Show *Three Trees*.) "Hmmm," said Brennan. "This tree is small. This tree is even smaller. This tree is the smallest of all, and since Max's mouse hole is very, very small, I'll take this tree to him."

Next, Brennan looked at stars for the top of the tree. (Show *Three Stars*.) "This star is small and this star is even smaller. This star is the smallest, so I'll take it. It will fit perfectly on Max's small tree."

Next, Brennan looked at lights. (Show *Christmas Lights*.) "These lights are small. These lights are even smaller, but these lights are the smallest. I think I'll buy the smallest lights."

The last thing Brennan looked at was ornaments. (Show *Christmas Ornaments*.) "These ornaments are small. These ornaments are even smaller, but these are the smallest. I'll buy the smallest Christmas ornaments for Max's tree.

Brennan took everything he had bought to Max's mouse hole. When Max saw Brennan coming, he said, "Brennan, you are terrific! Now I'll have a decorated tree for Christmas. Even though I have the chicken pox, I'll have a very happy Christmas. Thank you!"

Questions:

1. Who was Brennan's smallest friend?
2. Tell why Max was sad.
3. How long did Max have to stay in his mouse hole?
4. What did Brennan find to put on top of the tree?
5. Tell what Brennan bought.
6. Why did Brennan buy the smallest things?
7. Why was Max happy at the end of the story?
8. Why should you stay home if you have the chicken pox?
9. Why do some people decorate trees for Christmas?
10. What kind of things can we put on a Christmas tree?

Brennan's Friends

December: *small, smaller, smallest*

Three Trees

December: *small, smaller, smallest*

Three Stars

December: *small, smaller, smallest*

Christmas Lights

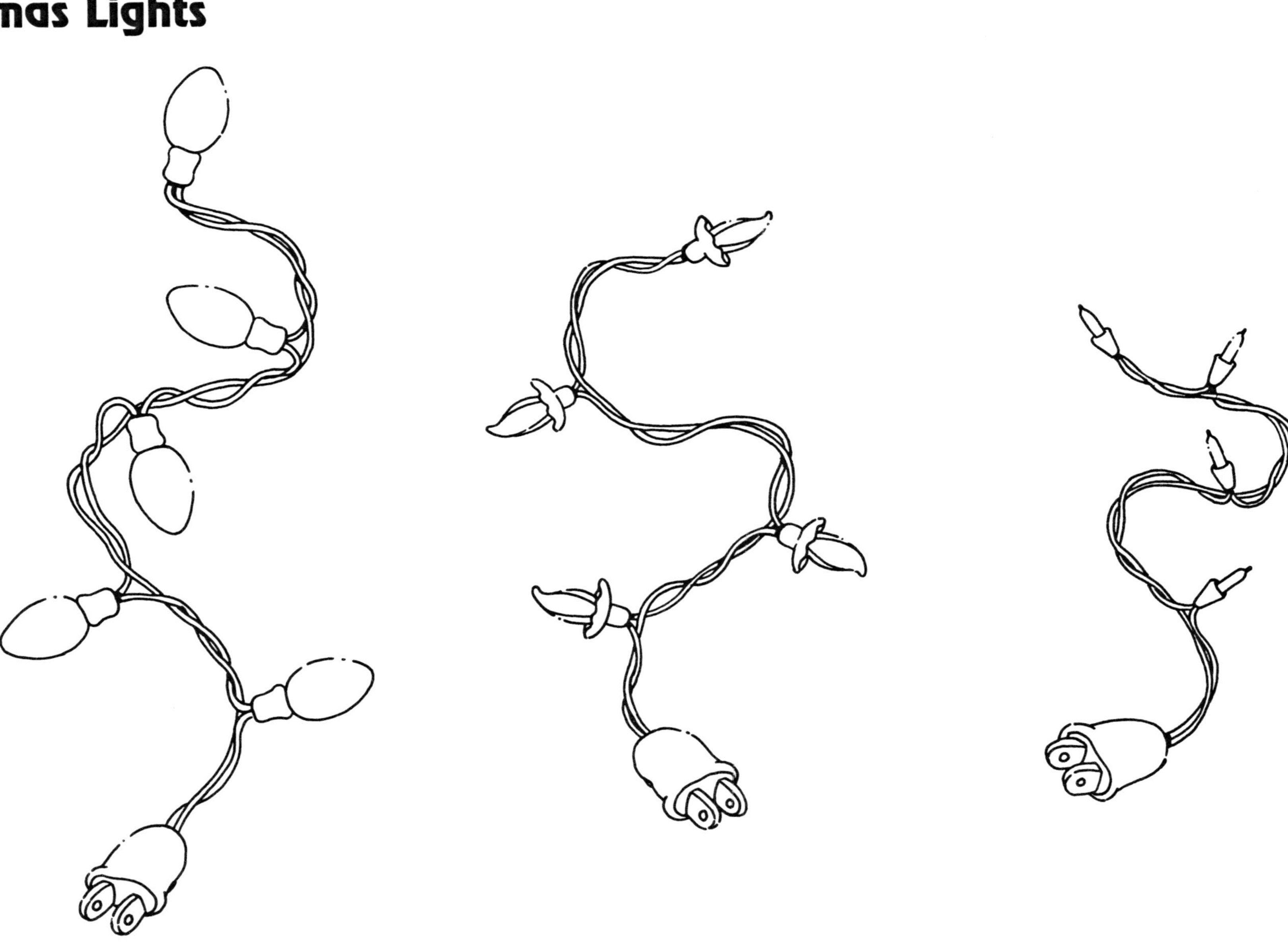

December: *small, smaller, smallest*

Christmas Ornaments

Holiday Lineup: Instructions

Give each child a copy of *Holiday Lineup*. Have the children listen carefully and follow your directions. Remind them to listen for the words *small*, *smaller*, and *smallest*.

1. Give the small angel a blue dress.
2. Draw a red line under the gift that's smaller than the bell.
3. Give the smallest candle an orange flame.
4. Color the toe of the small stocking green.
5. Color the smallest picture on the page gray.
6. Put orange polka dots on the smallest ornament.
7. Look at row three. Draw something in the box that's smaller than the star.
8. Color the ribbon on the smallest gift green.
9. Put a yellow check mark on each thing that's smaller than the star in row three.
10. Put a small red X on the tree in row one.
11. Put a purple X on the smallest picture in row one.
12. Put two red ornaments on the small tree.
13. Look at row one. Draw five small circles on one of the gifts.
14. Draw a green circle around the stocking that's smaller than both angels.
15. Draw a small star on the stocking in row two.

It must be time for Christmas!

Holiday Lineup

Name ______________________

1.

2.

3.

December: *small, smaller, smallest*

Star Student: Instructions

Discuss the words *nearest* and *farthest* with the children. Then, give a copy of *Star Student* to each child.

"Today, our star student Brennan wants to play a game with you. He has some questions for you. I'm going to ask some of you to answer these questions. If you answer a question correctly, the class gets a star. If your answer isn't right, Brennan gets the star. Do you think you can get more stars than Brennan?"

"Look at your picture of Brennan. Help me keep score by drawing a star under the word *Class* each time someone answers a question correctly, or under Brennan's name each time an answer is wrong."

When you're done, have the children count the number of stars under each heading to see how well the class did. Then, the children can color the worksheet and the stars.

1. Who is nearest the door?
2. Who is nearest the windows?
3. Who is farthest from the chalkboard?
4. What is nearest my desk?
5. What is farthest from the pencil sharpener?
6. Who is farthest from me?
7. Who is nearest a chalkboard eraser?
8. What is nearest the table?
9. Who is nearest (a student's name)?
10. Who is farthest from (a student's name)?
11. Who is nearest the wastebasket?
12. What is nearest the lights?
13. What is farthest from the ceiling?
14. Who is nearest the front wall?
15. What is nearest the clock?

You're the star students today!

Note: There may be more than one correct answer for each question. Accept all reasonable answers. In addition, you may need to alter the questions to suit your classroom arrangement.

Star Student

Name ______________________________

Class

Brennan

Ready for Christmas: Instructions

Give each child a copy of *Ready for Christmas*. Have the children listen carefully and follow your directions. Remind them to listen for the words *nearest* and *farthest*.

1. Give the bear farthest from the tree a red coat.
2. Color the bell nearest the small candy cane yellow.
3. Color the star nearest the bottom of the tree blue.
4. Color the candle farthest from the tree green.
5. Color the bell farthest from the small candy cane green.
6. Give the bear nearest the tree a blue hat.
7. Color the star farthest from the bells yellow.
8. Color the ornament nearest the top of the tree blue.
9. Give the bear farthest from the tree a purple hat.
10. Color the candle nearest the tree red.
11. Color the candle holder farthest from the tree yellow.
12. Color the ornament nearest the bottom of the tree purple.
13. Use a black crayon to write your name under the bear farthest from the tree.
14. Give the candle farthest from the gingerbread man an orange flame.
15. Give the bear nearest the tree purple boots.

It's going to be a wonderful Christmas for these bears!

Ready for Christmas

Name ______________________

December: *nearest, farthest*

Three Stockings

Directions: Divide your class into three groups. Have the groups sit in rows so you have a first group, a middle group, and a last group. Tell the groups you're going to read a story. Have the first group listen for the word *first* and clap once each time they hear their word. Have the middle group listen for the word *middle* and clap once each time they hear their word. Have the last group listen for the word *last* and clap once each time they hear their word. (You may want to practice a few times before you read the story.)

❄ ❄ ❄ ❄ ❄ ❄ ❄ ❄ ❄ ❄ ❄ ❄ ❄ ❄ ❄ ❄ ❄ ❄ ❄

Brennan has invited three of his friends to a Christmas party. The party is tomorrow and Brennan is very busy. He has just finished decorating his Christmas tree. Now, it's time to hang his friends' stockings over the fireplace.

Brennan hangs Sam Squirrel's stocking first. He puts Randy Raccoon's stocking in the middle. He hangs Rodney Rabbit's stocking last. "They look very pretty," says Brennan. "The first stocking is green, the middle stocking is white, and the last stocking is red."

"Oops!" exclaims Brennan. "I almost forgot to fill the stockings!" He quickly puts a sparkly Christmas ornament in each stocking. He puts a star ornament in the first stocking, a reindeer ornament in the middle stocking, and a bell ornament in the last stocking.

Finally, Brennan puts a gift in each stocking. He puts an acorn in the first stocking. "Sam will love that," says Brennan. He puts an ear of corn in the middle stocking. "Randy Raccoon loves corn," says Brennan. Then, he puts a carrot in the last stocking for Rodney Rabbit.

"Now," says Brennan, "the first stocking, the middle stocking, and the last stocking are filled. I'm ready for the party!"

Questions for each group:

1. Whose stocking was first/middle/last?
2. What color was the first/middle/last stocking?
3. What ornament did Brennan put in the first/middle/last stocking?
4. What gift did Brennan put in the first/middle/last stocking?

Note: For additional fun, have a child from each group draw the first, middle, or last stocking on the chalkboard. Encourage the children to put the stockings in the right order and add the appropriate ornaments and gifts.

Decorate the Christmas Trees: Instructions

Give each child a copy of *Decorate the Christmas Trees*. Have the children listen carefully and follow your directions. Remind them to listen for the words *first*, *middle*, and *last*.

1. Put two red balls on the first tree from Brennan.
2. Put a yellow star on top of the last tree from Brennan.
3. Color the middle pot orange.
4. Draw a blue ball on the middle tree.
5. Color the last pot from Brennan brown.
6. Color a red ball on the middle tree.
7. Put a blue ball and a yellow ball on the first tree from Brennan.
8. Draw a green ball on the middle tree.
9. Put a purple ball on the first tree from Brennan.
10. Draw two yellow balls on the middle tree.
11. Put a blue star on top of the first tree from Brennan.
12. Put two orange balls on the last tree from Brennan.
13. Draw a red star on top of the middle tree.
14. Color a yellow ball on the last tree from Brennan.
15. Color the first pot from Brennan purple.

What colorful Christmas trees!

Decorate the Christmas Trees

Name ______________________

Home Lesson

Dear ________________,

During the month of December, we have been working on these concepts: *behind*, *in front of*, *first*, *middle*, *last*, *nearest*, *farthest*, *small*, *smaller*, and *smallest*. You can help your child review these concepts by giving your child the sheet attached to this page. Read the directions below and encourage your child to listen carefully and follow your directions. Here are the materials you will need: a box of eight crayons, a table, a chair, and a quiet place to work.

Directions:

1. Draw two oranges in the first stocking from the spider.
2. Color the log farthest from the flames black.
3. Circle the mouse nearest the logs with your purple crayon.
4. Look at the middle stocking. Color the smallest ball blue.
5. Draw a red apple behind the truck.
6. Put a yellow check mark over the middle candy cane.
7. Put a small green present in front of the sleeping mouse.
8. Find the mittens. Color the smaller mitten yellow.
9. Draw a red circle around the mouse that is farthest from the logs.
10. Color the smallest candy cane green.
11. Put one blue present in front of the fireplace.
12. Color the small log brown.
13. Put an orange X on the first candy cane from the spider.
14. Draw a yellow star on the middle stocking.
15. Color the last candy cane from the spider red.

Thank you for your help. Have a wonderful holiday!

Sincerely,

____

Name ______________________________

ZZZ

Bear Head: Instructions

Give each child two copies of *Bear Head*. Ask the children if the bear heads are the same or different. Then, have the children listen carefully and follow your directions. Remind them to listen for the words *same* and *different*.

1. Draw eyes on the bears so they look the same.
2. Draw different noses on the bears.
3. Draw different mouths on the bears.
4. Give the bears hats that are the same.
5. Add something to each hat so they look different.
6. Give the bears ties that are the same shape, but different colors.

How are the bears the same? How are they different?

Bear Head

Name ______________________________

Winter Fun: Instructions

Give each child a copy of *Winter Fun*. Have the children listen carefully and follow your directions. Remind them to listen for the words *same* and *different*.

Look at box one.

1. Color the bears that are the same brown.
2. Color the different bear's belt black.

Look at box two.

1. Put a red circle around the different snowflake.
2. Color the same snowflakes blue.

Look at box three.

1. Color the small presents the same color.
2. Use a different color to color the big presents.

Look at box four.

1. Color the hats that are the same green.
2. Put a purple feather in the different hat.

Look at box five.

1. Find the gloves that are the same. Color them yellow.
2. Color the gloves that are different green and red.

Look at box six.

1. Color the different thing green.
2. Put a red X on the things that are the same.

Look at box seven.

1. Color the hats on the snowmen that are the same blue.
2. Give the different snowman a purple scarf.

Look at box eight.

1. Color the cats that are the same orange.
2. Color the different cats yellow.

Good job! We sure have a lot of fun in the winter!

Winter Fun

Name ______________________

Smiling Bears: Instructions

Directions: Draw three rectangles on the chalkboard. Make the first rectangle the narrowest, the next rectangle wider, and the last rectangle the widest. Ask a child to put an X on the widest rectangle. Then, have him tell what he did. Next, have another child draw a line through the narrowest rectangle. Encourage him to tell what he did. Have the children discuss the words *widest* and *narrowest*.

When the children seem to understand the concepts of *widest* and *narrowest*, give each child a copy of *Smiling Bears*. Encourage the children to listen carefully and follow your directions so they can draw faces on the bears.

1. Give the widest bear blue eyes.
2. Give an ice cream cone to the bear that's the narrowest.
3. Give the bear that isn't the widest or the narrowest a brown nose.
4. Give the widest bear a black nose.
5. Draw a red smile on the widest bear's face.
6. Give the bear that isn't the widest or the narrowest a basketball to hold.
7. Give the narrowest bear brown eyes.
8. Give the widest bear a race car to hold.
9. Color the narrowest bear's ears black.
10. Use a yellow crayon to color the ears of the bear that isn't the widest or the narrowest.
11. Draw an orange smile on the narrowest bear's face.
12. Give the narrowest bear a red nose.
13. Give the bear that isn't the widest or the narrowest green eyes.
14. Color the widest bear's ears red.
15. Draw a brown smile on the face of the bear that isn't the widest or the narrowest.

Which smiling bear do you like best?

Smiling Bears

Name ______________________

January: *widest, narrowest*

Snowmen: Instructions

Give each child a copy of *Snowmen*. Have the children listen carefully and follow your directions. Remind them to listen for the words *widest* and *narrowest*.

1. Put a black hat on the narrowest snowman.
2. Put three green buttons on the widest snowman.
3. Put brown stick arms on the widest snowman and the narrowest snowman.
4. Give the narrowest snowman two banana ears.
5. Put black stick arms on the snowman that isn't the widest or the narrowest.
6. Put an orange scarf on the widest snowman.
7. Draw an orange broom beside the narrowest snowman.
8. Put a red hat on the snowman that isn't the widest or the narrowest.
9. Draw a purple shovel beside the widest snowman.
10. Put a blue scarf on the narrowest snowman.
11. Put a yellow hat on the widest snowman.
12. Put five black buttons on the snowman that isn't the widest or the narrowest.
13. Put a green scarf on the snowman that isn't the widest or the narrowest.
14. Give the widest snowman two carrot ears.
15. Put four red buttons on the narrowest snowman.

You made some colorful snowmen!

Snowmen

Name ____________________

January: *widest, narrowest*

Disappearing Bears

Directions: Draw the bear on the following page twice on your chalkboard. Draw one bear on the right side of the chalkboard and one bear on the left side. Then, discuss the concepts of *left* and *right* with the children, referring to the bears.

When the children understand the concepts, tell them that the bears are magic. They can disappear, but they need the children's help. Ask the children to listen carefully and follow your directions to make the bears disappear. Have the children take turns following your instructions, using a chalkboard eraser.

1. Erase one leg and foot of the right bear.
2. Erase one arm and paw of the left bear.
3. Erase the right bear's mouth.
4. Erase one of the right bear's ears.
5. Erase both of the left bear's eyes.
6. Erase the left bear's nose.
7. Erase one arm and paw of the right bear.
8. Erase one leg and foot of the left bear.
9. Erase the right bear's nose.
10. Erase the right bear's ear.
11. Erase the left bear's mouth.
12. Erase a leg and foot from each bear.
13. Erase the eyes of the right bear.
14. Erase the only ears on the board.
15. Erase the right bear's arm and paw.
16. Erase the left bear's head.
17. Erase the right bear's body.
18. Erase the only arm and paw on the board.
19. Erase the only head on the board.
20. Erase the only body on the board.

What a great disappearing act!

Disappearing Bears, continued

Directions: Draw the bear below twice on your chalkboard. Draw one bear on the right side of the chalkboard and one bear on the left side. Then, follow the instructions on the previous page to help the children understand the concepts of *left* and *right*, and to make the bears disappear from the chalkboard.

Bundle-a-Bear: Instructions

Give each child a copy of *Bundle-a-Bear*. Have the children listen carefully and follow your directions. Remind them to listen for the words *left* and *right*.

1. Put a red hat on the bear that's on the right.
2. Put a pair of blue mittens on the left bear.
3. Give the bear on the left orange boots.
4. Put a pair of black boots on the bear that's on the right.
5. Give the bear on the right a pair of green mittens.
6. Give the left bear blue pants.
7. Give the bear on the right a red scarf.
8. Put a blue hat on the bear on the left.
9. Put a red coat on the bear that's on the left.
10. Give the right bear green pants.
11. Give the left bear a purple scarf.
12. Put a yellow coat on the bear that's on the right.

Now, the bears are ready to build a snowman!

Bundle-a-Bear

Name ________________________

Brennan Visits the Circus

Directions: Encourage the children to listen carefully as you read the story below. After you read the story, ask the children the questions listed at the bottom of the page.

❄ ❄ ❄ ❄ ❄ ❄ ❄ ❄ ❄ ❄ ❄ ❄ ❄ ❄ ❄ ❄ ❄ ❄ ❄

Brennan Bear and his friends Kari Cat and Dennis Dog were very excited. They were going to the circus after school. All day they were wiggly and they had a hard time paying attention to their teacher. Finally, the school bell rang and they were off to the circus.

As they got near the circus tent, Brennan pushed Kari and Dennis out of the way and ran ahead. "Me first, me first!" he shouted.

Kari and Dennis weren't very happy. "Hey, Brennan," said Dennis, "it's not very nice to push and shove and always be first."

"It's okay, Brennan," said Kari. "I have an idea. Let's take turns being first. You can go first to get your ticket, Dennis can go second, and I'll go third. The next time, someone else can go first." Everyone thought this was a good plan.

"I'm hungry," said Dennis. "Let's get some popcorn!" Brennan, Kari, and Dennis skipped over to the popcorn stand. "Dennis, you can buy your popcorn first," said Brennan. "Kari can go second, and I'll go third."

After everyone bought popcorn, they went into the tent. There was so much to see — elephants, clowns, horses, and tightrope walkers. Brennan, Kari, and Dennis sat in the first row. A clown came by, selling pretty balloons. "I just love balloons!" said Kari. "Let's buy one."

"You can go first, Kari," said Dennis. "Brennan can buy his balloon second, and I'll go third." They each bought a balloon, then sat down to watch the show.

Brennan, Kari, and Dennis had a wonderful time that afternoon. The circus was great, but the best part of the day was being with each other.

Questions:

1. Name Brennan's friends.
2. Where did Brennan and his friends go?
3. How did Brennan, Kari, and Dennis decide who got to do things first?
4. Who was first to get a ticket to the circus?
5. What did Brennan, Kari, and Dennis see at the circus?
6. Who was selling the balloons?
7. What would you do if you didn't have enough money to buy a balloon?
8. Where is another place you could see elephants?
9. Would you rather be first, second, or third in line? Why?
10. Describe your favorite circus act.

Brennan, Kari, and Dennis: Instructions

Give each child a copy of *Brennan, Kari, and Dennis*. Have the children listen carefully and follow your directions. Remind them to listen for the words *first*, *second*, and *third*.

1. Give the first animal in line a blue tie.
2. Give the second animal in line a red bow on its tail.
3. Give the third animal in line brown shoes.
4. Give the third animal in line a green baseball cap.
5. Put a red collar on the second animal in line.
6. Give the second animal in line blue shoes.
7. Put a black number 1 under the first animal in line.
8. Who was the first animal in the story to get a circus ticket? Draw a purple ticket in his balloon.
9. Give the first animal in line a blue hat.
10. Who was the first animal in the story to get popcorn at the circus? Draw some yellow popcorn in his balloon.
11. Put a black number 2 under the second animal in line.
12. Color the second animal in line orange.
13. Who was the first animal in the story to get a balloon at the circus? Color that animal's balloon red.
14. Put a black number 3 under the third animal in line.
15. Give the third animal in line a green collar.

Brennan, Kari, and Dennis sure had fun at the circus, didn't they?

Note: Feel free to review the story or parts of it to help the children remember who did things first, second, and third.

Brennan, Kari, and Dennis

Name ______________________

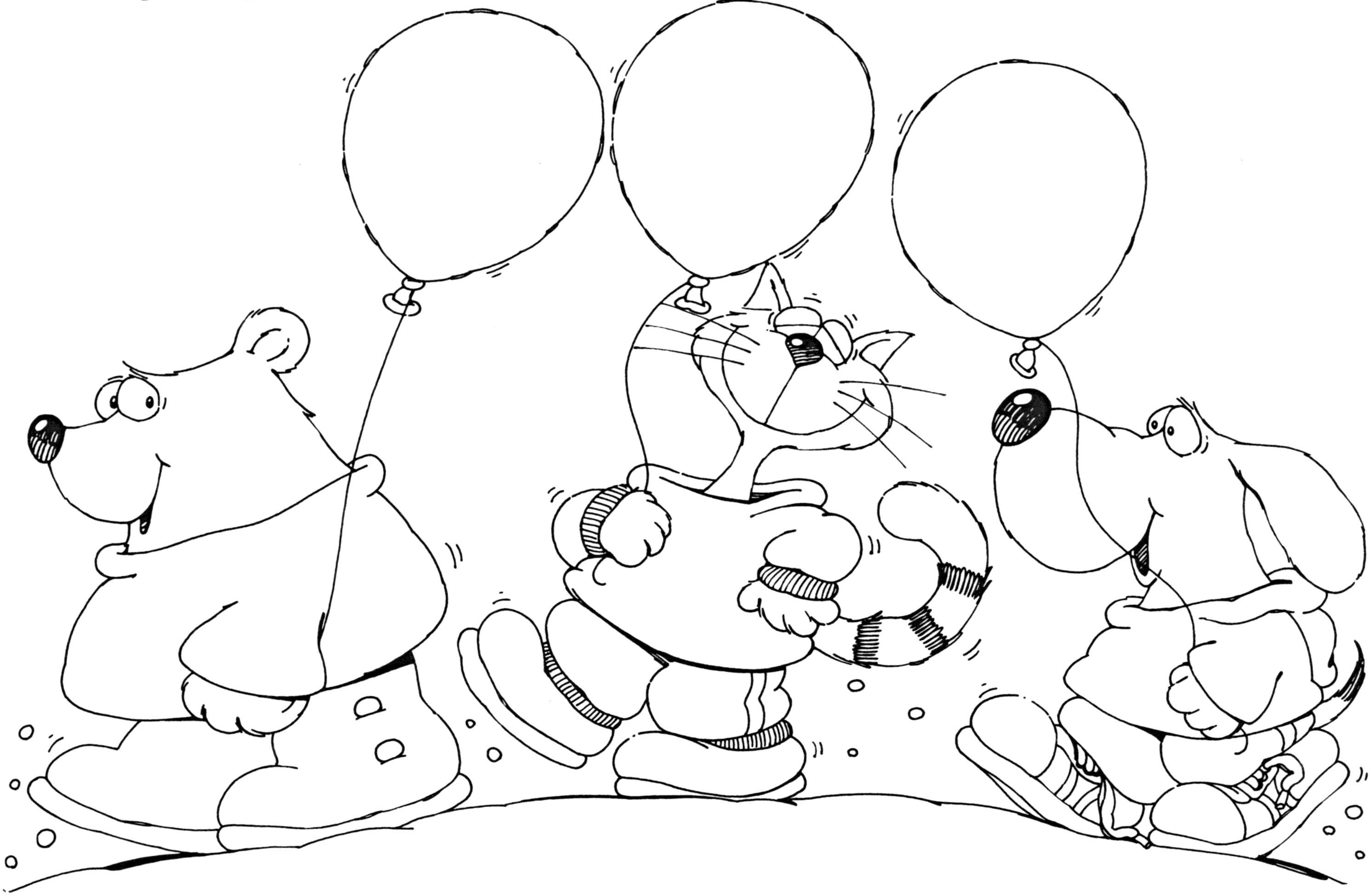

Brennan's Birthday: Instructions

Give each child a copy of *Brennan's Birthday*. Then, read the story below. Have the children listen carefully and follow your directions to find out Brennan's age. Remind the children to listen for the word *skip*.

❄ ❄ ❄ ❄ ❄ ❄ ❄ ❄ ❄ ❄ ❄ ❄ ❄ ❄ ❄ ❄ ❄ ❄ ❄

It was Brennan's birthday. He was very excited because he was going to have a birthday party. He had invited four friends to his party and his mom had baked his favorite cake — a honey bee cake. Yum!

When Brennan's friends arrived for the party, they brought Brennan gifts. All of Brennan's friends wanted to know how old Brennan was, but Brennan wouldn't tell them. He told them they were going to play a listening game to find out how old he was. He gave each of his friends a piece of paper that looked like this. (Hold up a copy of *Brennan's Birthday*.)

Let's follow the directions Brennan gave his friends to see if we can find out Brennan's age. When I read the directions, make sure you go in the same direction as the arrow at the top of your page.

1. Look at row one. Find the house. Skip a box and color in the next two boxes.

2. Look at row two. Find the ball. Skip a box and color in the next box.

3. Look at row three. Find the apple. Skip a box and color in the next box.

4. Look at row four. Find the circle. Skip a box and color in the next box.

5. Look at row five. Find the X. Skip a box and color in the next box. Stay in row five. Find the letter *B*. Skip a box and color in the next box.

6. Look at row six. Find the sun. Skip a box and color in the next box. Stay in row six. Find the box you just colored. Skip a box and color in the next box. Stay in row six. Find the second box you colored. Skip a box and color in the next box.

7. Look at row seven. Find the balloon. Skip a box and color in the next two boxes. Stay in row seven. Find the ice cream cone. Skip a box and color in the next box.

8. Look at row eight. Find the tree. Skip a box and color in the next box. Stay in row eight. Find the flower. Skip two boxes and color in the next box.

9. Look at row nine. Find the letter *N*. Skip a box and color in the next three boxes.

Now, look at what you drew. How old is Brennan?

Brennan's Birthday

Name ______________________

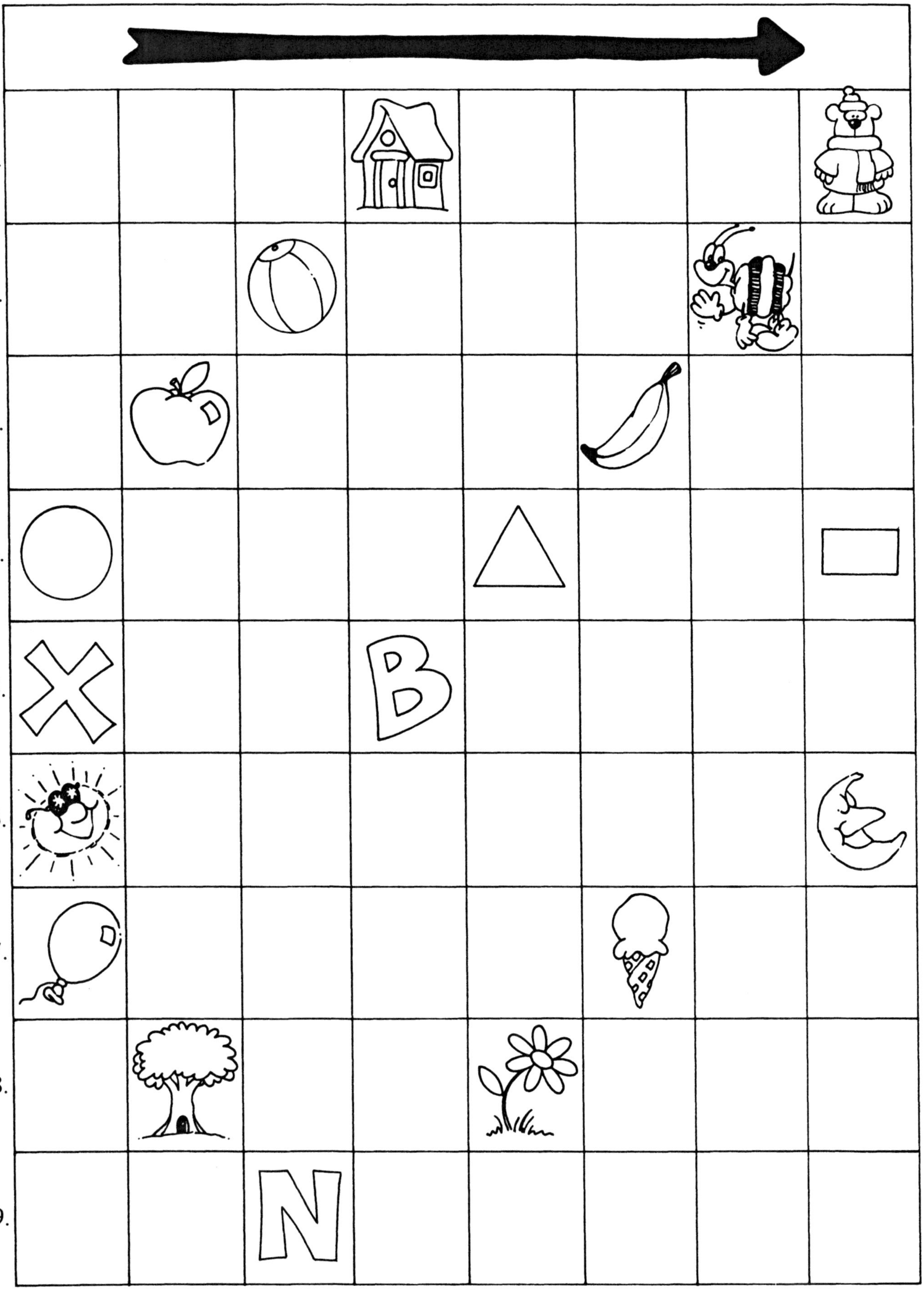

1.								
2.								
3.								
4.								
5.				B				
6.								
7.								
8.								
9.			N					

Birthday Treats: Instructions

Give each child a copy of *Birthday Treats*. Have the children listen carefully and follow your directions, going in the direction of the arrow at the top of their worksheet. Remind them to listen for the word *skip*.

Look at row one.

1. Look at the birthday card. Skip a box and draw a blue balloon.
2. Look at the candle. Skip a box and draw a red smiley face.

Look at row two.

1. Find the cake with one candle. Skip a box and draw a yellow sun.
2. Find the cake with two candles. Skip a box and draw a purple X.

Look at row three.

1. Find the party hat. Skip a box and draw a brown spider.
2. Find the present. Skip a box and draw another present with a green crayon.

Look at row four.

1. Find the dish of ice cream. Skip two boxes and draw an orange candle that's burning.
2. Find the ice cream cone. Skip a box and draw a black triangle.

Look at row five.

1. Find the bear with the party hat. Skip a box and draw a red pencil.
2. Find the bear that doesn't have a hat. Skip a box and use a blue crayon to write how old you are.

Brennan says, "Thank you for a fun birthday!"

Birthday Treats

Name ______________________

January: *skip*

Home Lesson

Dear ________________,

During the month of January, we have been working on these concepts: *same*, *different*, *widest*, *narrowest*, *left*, *right*, *first*, *second*, *third*, and *skip*. You can help your child review these concepts by giving your child the sheet attached to this page. Read the directions below and encourage your child to listen carefully and follow your directions. Here are the materials you will need: a box of eight crayons, a table, a chair, and a quiet place to work.

Directions:

1. Put a red scarf on the second snowman in line.
2. Put a yellow hat on the widest snowman.
3. Put blue mittens on the snowman on the left.
4. Put an orange scarf on the third snowman in line.
5. Put two green buttons on the narrowest snowman. Skip a snowman and draw two green buttons on that snowman.
6. Draw two different colored buttons on the second snowman in line.
7. Put a black hat on the first snowman in line.
8. Put brown mittens on the snowman that's on the right. Put the same color mittens on the second snowman in line.
9. Put a purple scarf on the snowman that's on the left.
10. Draw two blue snowflakes above the snowman that's the widest.

Happy New Year!

Sincerely,

____

Name ______________________

Follow Me

Directions: Have the children stand in a half circle facing you. Encourage the children to listen carefully and follow your directions. Remind them to listen for the words *above* and *below*.

For additional practice, have the children make up commands using the words *above* and *below*.

1. Put your hands above your head.
2. Put your hands above your shoulders.
3. Put your thumbs below your chin.
4. Put your left hand above your left ear.
5. Put your right hand below your nose.
6. Put your hands below your knees.
7. Put your hands above your feet.
8. Put your hands above your eyes.
9. Put your left hand above your right hand.
10. Put your left hand below your nose.
11. Put your right hand above your left wrist.
12. Put your hands above your knees.
13. Put your fingers below your eyes.
14. Put your right hand above your heart.
15. Put your left hand below your right hand.
16. Put your elbows above your knees.
17. Put your hands below your ears.
18. Put your right foot above your left foot.
19. Put your thumbs below your knees.
20. Put your right hand above your right ear.

Valentine Hearts: Instructions

Give each child a copy of *Valentine Hearts*. Have the children listen carefully and follow your directions. Remind them to listen for the words *above* and *below*.

1. Draw a red heart in the box above Cupid.
2. Draw a blue heart in the box above the flowers.
3. Draw a brown heart in the box below the candy.
4. Draw a purple heart in the box above the letter.
5. Put a black X in the box below the flowers.
6. Draw a blue heart in the box below Cupid.
7. Draw a red heart in the box above the heart with an arrow.
8. Draw a green heart in the box below the broken heart.
9. Draw a yellow heart in the box above the candy.
10. Draw a yellow circle around the heart above the green heart.
11. Draw an orange line through the picture below the purple heart.
12. Draw a purple circle around the picture above the black X.
13. Draw a green line through the heart below Cupid.
14. Put an orange X on the picture above the brown heart.
15. Draw a purple smiley face in the heart below the broken heart.

What beautiful hearts you drew!

Valentine Hearts

Name ______________________

From A Friend
To My Valentine

Brennan Visits the Mall

Directions: Give a copy of *The Mall* to each child. Talk about the stores and where they're located — on a side, in the center, or in a corner. Then, encourage the children to listen as you read a story about Brennan going to the mall. Have the children trace Brennan's route on their maps as you tell the story. Remind the children to listen for the words *corner*, *center*, and *side*.

❄ ❄ ❄ ❄ ❄ ❄ ❄ ❄ ❄ ❄ ❄ ❄ ❄ ❄ ❄ ❄ ❄ ❄ ❄

Brennan was acting very funny. He asked his mom if she would drive him to the mall. "Why do you want to go to the mall?" asked his mom.

"It's a secret," said Brennan, and his face turned very red.

"Okay, Brennan. Let's go," said his mom.

When they arrived at the mall, Brennan quickly jumped from the car. He opened the center door and looked around. He walked up one side of the mall to Sandie's Candies. He went inside the store and looked around. He had butterflies in his stomach as he bought a big, heart-shaped box of candy.

"I need a card, now," thought Brennan. He felt shaky inside as he walked around the corner to the map in the center of the mall. He wanted to buy a Valentine card, but he didn't know where the card shop was. He looked at the map of the mall and found Kari's Card Shop. It was on the other side of the mall.

Brennan walked past the corner store and then went into Kari's Card Shop. He felt a tingly, warm feeling as he bought a lacy, red Valentine card.

After Brennan was finished shopping, he walked down the side of the mall and out the center door. His mom was waiting for him in the car. "Hi, Brennan. What did you buy?" asked his mom.

"Oh, nothing much," answered Brennan with a smile.

Brennan's mom began to smile, too. "I think I know why you've been acting so funny," she said. "I think you have a girlfriend!"

Brennan's face turned red. "It sure is hard to keep a secret from you, Mom!"

Questions:

1. Where did Brennan want to go?
2. Which door did Brennan walk through to go into the mall?
3. Where was Sandie's Candies in the mall?
4. What two things did Brennan buy?
5. Why was Brennan acting so funny?
6. What do you do in a mall?
7. Name some different kinds of candies.
8. What other things could you buy at a card shop?
9. Mix up the letters in the word "map" to find out Brennan's girlfriend's name.
10. Who is your favorite Valentine? Why?

The Mall

Name ______________________

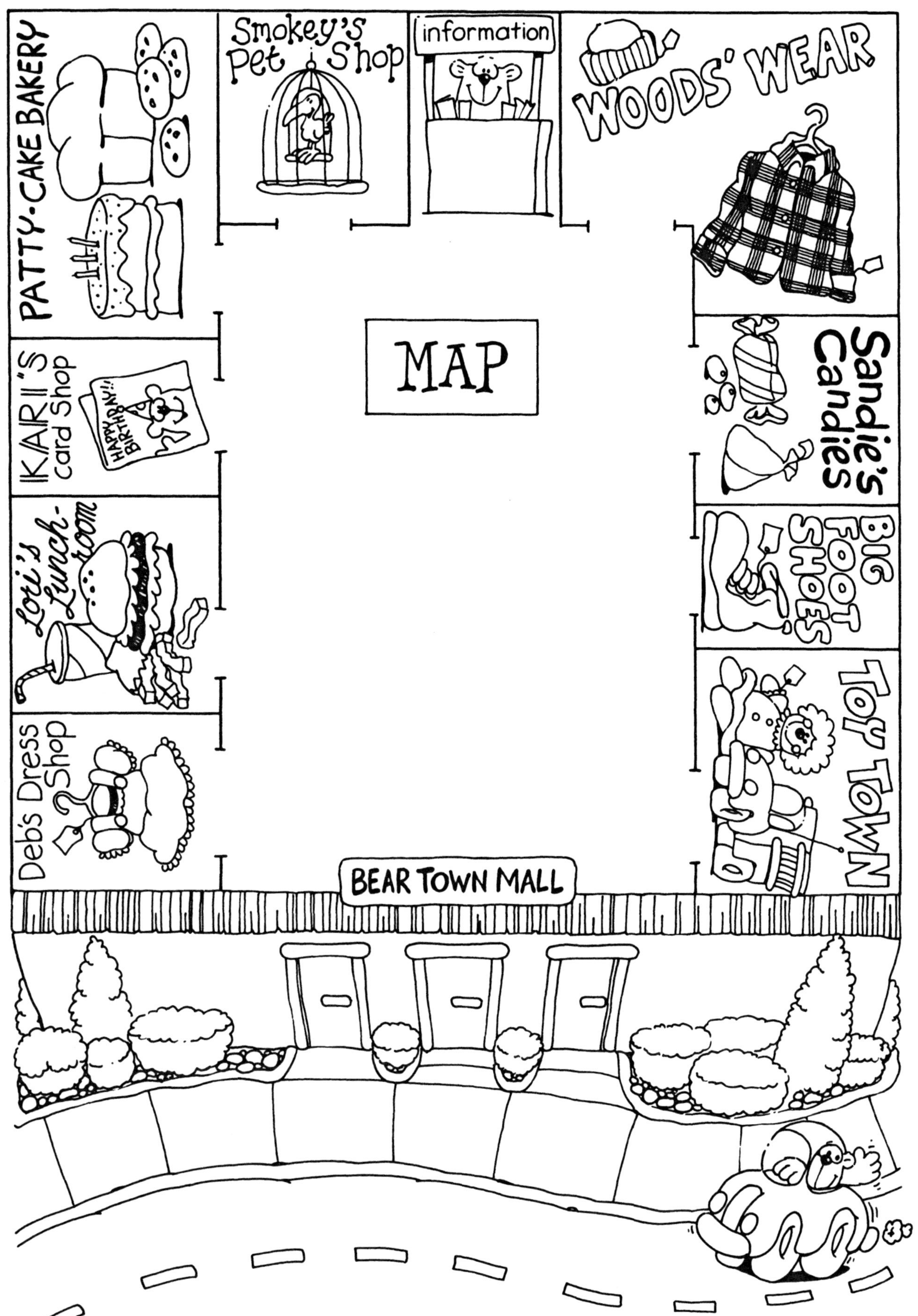

The Valentine Shop: Instructions

Give each child a copy of *The Valentine Shop*. Have the children listen carefully and follow your directions. Remind them to listen for the words *corner*, *center*, and *side*.

1. Draw a red heart in the middle of the center shelf.
2. Draw two yellow hearts on one side of the top shelf.
3. Draw a purple heart in a corner of the top shelf.
4. Draw a brown box of candy in the center of the bottom shelf.
5. Draw a green ball on the right side of the middle shelf.
6. Draw a red Valentine card in a corner of the bottom shelf.
7. Draw a blue arrow on one side of the teddy bear.
8. Write your name with black in the center of the bear's heart.
9. Draw a green heart in the center of the top shelf.
10. Draw two orange hearts on the center shelf.
11. Color the left side of the bookcase yellow.
12. Put a black spider in a corner on the middle shelf.
13. Draw a small purple heart on either side of the ball.
14. Draw a gray cobweb in a corner on the bottom shelf.
15. Color the right side of the bookcase brown.

What a nice place to shop for Valentine's Day!

The Valentine Shop

Name ___________________________

Presidents

Directions: Encourage the children to listen carefully as you read the stories below. Remind them to listen for the words *many*, *few*, and *no*. After you read each story, ask the children the questions listed at the bottom of the page.

George Washington

George Washington was the first president of the United States. He was very honest, even when he was a small boy. One day, when he was a little boy, George walked out to the garden where a cherry tree grew. It was a small tree with few cherries on it. George had just gotten a new ax and he wanted to see how well it worked. He decided to chop down the cherry tree. He chopped and chopped. He had to swing the ax many times to chop down the tree. When his father came home, he saw the cherry tree and was mad. "Who chopped down this cherry tree?" he shouted. George was scared, but he couldn't tell a lie. "I chopped it down, Father, and now I'm sad because we will have no cherries to make a cherry pie." George's father knew that George was very sorry and he said, "You won't be punished, George, because you told me the truth and that is important!"

Abraham Lincoln

Abraham Lincoln was very poor when he was a boy. There were no schools, but he wanted to learn. His mother helped him learn to read by the light from the fireplace. Abe loved to read and learn, but his family only had a few books. He wanted to learn so badly that he walked many miles to borrow books from his neighbors. He was very careful to take care of the books he borrowed and he always returned them. He grew up to be a great man and the sixteenth president of the United States.

Questions:

1. Who was George Washington?
2. What did George chop down?
3. How many cherries were on the cherry tree?
4. How many swings did it take to chop down the tree?
5. Tell why George was sad.
6. What did George's father do?
7. Name some other kinds of pies.
8. Do you think it's ever okay to tell a lie? Why or why not?

1. Did Abraham Lincoln have a lot of money?
2. How many schools were there when Abe was a boy?
3. Who helped Abe learn to read?
4. How many books did Abe's family have?
5. Tell how far Abe walked to borrow books.
6. How did Abe treat the books?
7. What are some other ways we learn besides reading books?
8. Would you like to be the president some day? Why or why not?

Fantastic February: Instructions

Give each child a copy of *Fantastic February*. Have the children listen carefully and follow your directions. Remind them to listen for the words *many*, *few*, and *no*.

Look at box one.

1. Find a tree with a few cherries. Color those cherries red.
2. Draw a bluebird in the tree with no cherries.

Look at box two.

1. Draw a purple circle around the coat with many buttons.
2. Put a green pocket on the coat with a few buttons.

Look at box three.

1. Color the wig with no curls brown.
2. Color the wig with many curls black.

Look at box four.

1. Put an orange X on the flag with a few stripes.
2. Color the stars on the flag with no stripes yellow.

Look at box five.

1. Draw a brown chimney on the house made of many logs.
2. Draw a red flower beside the house made of no logs.

Look at box six.

1. Draw two blue books on the shelf with a few books.
2. Draw a red apple on the shelf with many books.

Look at box seven.

1. Put a purple X on the bag with a few coins.
2. Draw a red smiley face on the bag with no coins.

Look at box eight.

1. Draw a yellow line above the ax with a few stripes.
2. Draw a brown log under the ax with no stripes.

You did a good job of listening!

Fantastic February

Name ___________________________

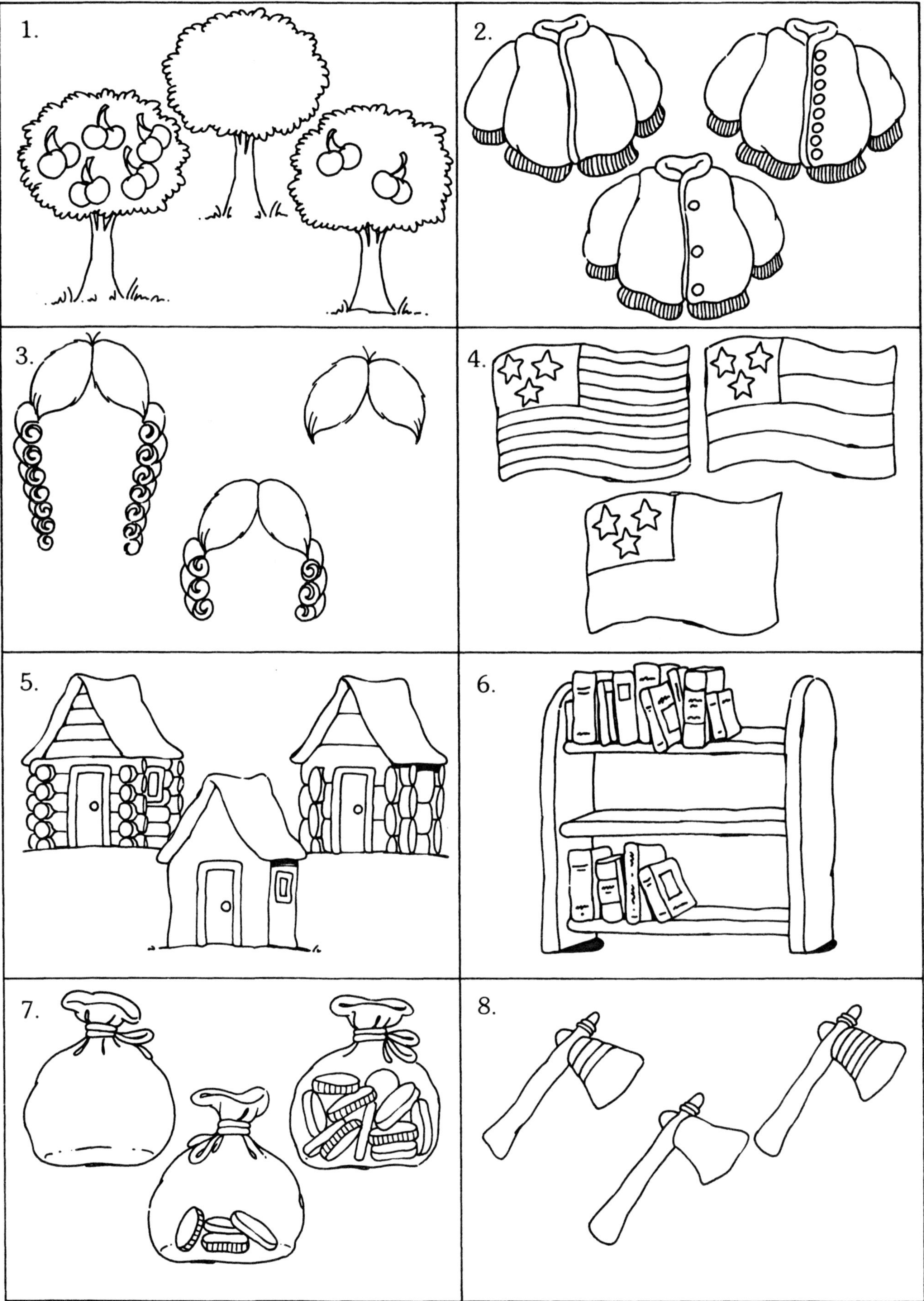

Everything Big

Directions: Tell the children you're going to read a story. Ask them to listen for the words *big*, *medium-sized*, and *small*. Each time they hear you say any of these words, they should raise their hands in the air.

❄ ❄ ❄ ❄ ❄ ❄ ❄ ❄ ❄ ❄ ❄ ❄ ❄ ❄ ❄ ❄ ❄ ❄ ❄

Brennan went to visit his friend Bernie. Bernie's dad had invited Brennan to go shopping with him and Bernie and to stay for supper. Brennan was glad he got to go shopping with them.

On their shopping trip, Bernie, his dad, and Brennan went into the toy store. Bernie and Brennan looked at toy trucks. Brennan picked up a tow truck and a pickup truck. He thought they were really neat.

Bernie saw what Brennan was holding and he said, "The pickup truck is small and the tow truck is medium-sized, but I want a big truck." So, Bernie picked out a big truck — a semitrailer.

Next, Brennan and Bernie looked at balls. Brennan liked the baseballs and the volleyballs. When Bernie saw the balls Brennan was holding, he said, "The baseball is small and the volleyball is medium-sized, but I'm going to buy the beach ball because it's a big ball."

Then, Bernie and Brennan looked at stuffed animals. Brennan liked the stuffed lion and the stuffed hippo. Bernie said to Brennan, "The stuffed lion is small and the stuffed hippo is medium-sized, but I want a big stuffed animal. I think I'll buy the stuffed elephant."

The last thing they looked at was coloring books. Brennan picked out a small book and a medium-sized book. Bernie picked out a different book — a big book, of course!

When they got home, Bernie's dad fixed supper — spinach. He gave Brennan a small plate of spinach and Bernie a big plate of spinach. Bernie's dad said, "Bernie, since you like everything big, you can have the big plate of spinach!"

Oh boy, poor Bernie!

Questions:

1. Who went shopping?
2. Tell what kind of store Bernie, his dad, and Brennan went to.
3. What toys did Brennan and Bernie look at?
4. What sizes of toys did Brennan pick out?
5. What size of toys did Bernie pick out?
6. Tell why Bernie got the big plate of spinach.
7. Do you think it's always better to have something big? Why or why not?
8. What's another word for *big*?
9. Who had more to carry if Bernie bought four big toys and Brennan bought four small and medium-sized toys?
10. Name something you would like to have that's small.

Toy Box Fun: Instructions

Give each child a copy of *Toy Box Fun*. Have the children listen carefully and follow your directions. Remind them to listen for the words *big*, *medium-sized*, and *small*.

Look at the toy box with trucks in it.

1. Put a red X on the truck that's big.
2. Draw a purple line through the medium-sized truck.
3. Draw a blue circle around the small truck.

Look at the toy box with balls in it.

1. Put a green X on the medium-sized ball.
2. Draw an orange line above the small ball.
3. Color the big ball yellow.

Look at the toy box with stuffed animals in it.

1. Draw a red square around the small stuffed animal.
2. Draw a black line through the big stuffed animal.
3. Draw a brown circle around the medium-sized stuffed animal.

Look at the toy box with the books in it.

1. Draw a blue line below the medium-sized book.
2. Color the big book purple.
3. Draw an orange circle above the small book.

Now, look at Brennan and Bernie. Can you tell which bear is Bernie? He doesn't look very happy! Give Bernie and Brennan some green spinach on their plates. Make sure Bernie has the big plate of spinach.

Toy Box Fun

Name ______________________

Home Lesson

Dear ________________,

During the month of February, we have been working on these concepts: *above*, *below*, *corner*, *center*, *side*, *many*, *few*, *no*, *big*, *medium-sized*, and *small*. You can help your child review these concepts by giving your child the sheet attached to this page. Read the directions below and encourage your child to listen carefully and follow your directions. Here are the materials you will need: a box of eight crayons, a table, a chair, and a quiet place to work.

Directions:

1. Look at the envelopes below the mailbox. Color the envelope with many hearts red. Color the envelope with no hearts blue. Color the envelope with a few hearts purple.
2. Draw a yellow bow in the center of the mailbox pole.
3. Draw three green hearts in a corner of the mailbox.
4. Color the big arrow on the ground blue.
5. Draw a black arrow below Cupid.
6. Draw a purple heart in the center of the mailbox.
7. Draw a big red heart on one side of the purple heart.
8. Draw one brown arrow above Cupid.
9. Color the tip of the small arrow on the ground red.
10. Circle the medium-sized arrow on the ground with a purple crayon.
11. Draw a few orange hearts hanging from strings below the mailbox.
12. Draw a blue curvy line above the yellow bow.

I appreciate your help. Thank you!

Sincerely,

____

Name ___________________________

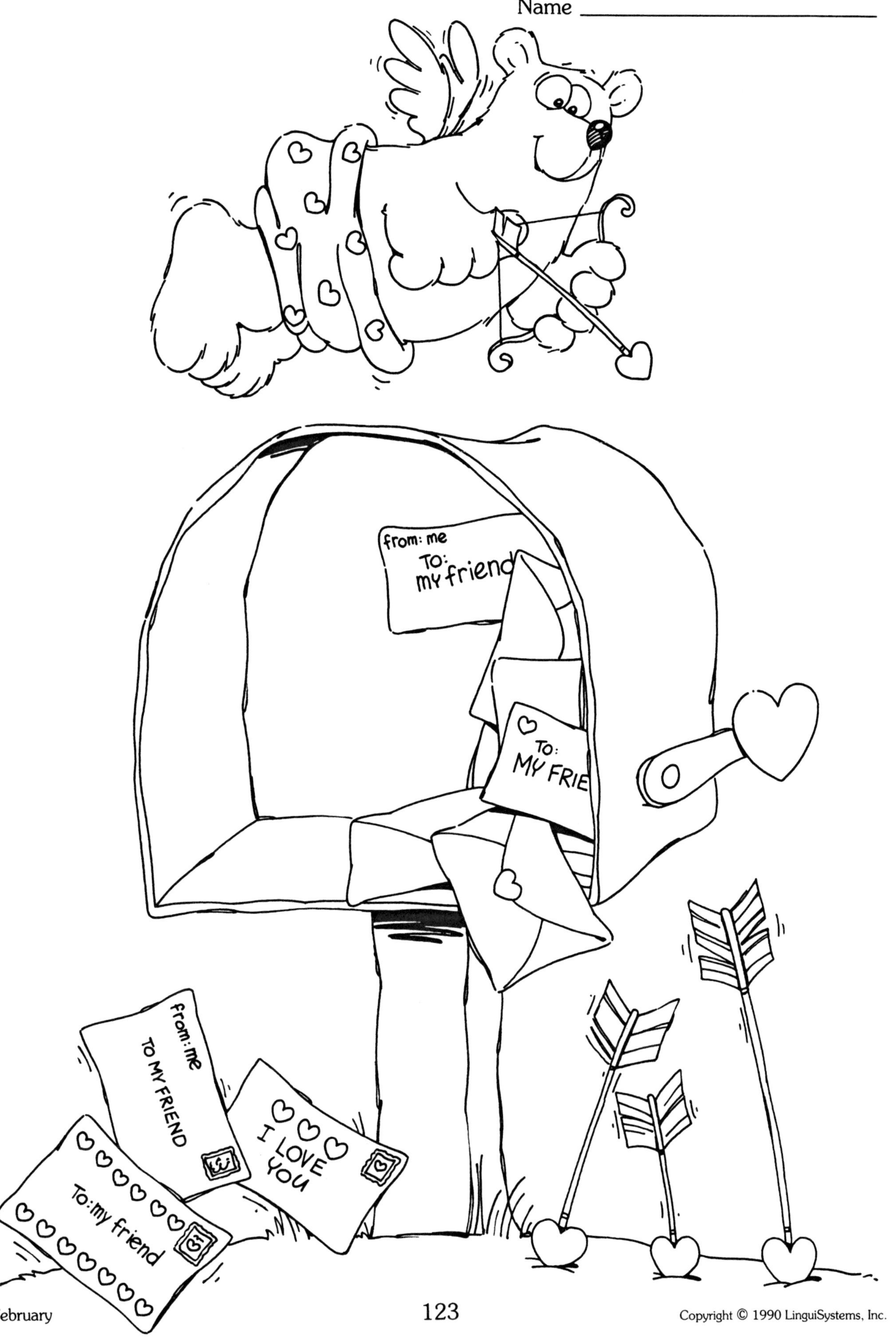

from: me
TO:
my friend
TO:
MY FRIE
from: me
TO MY FRIEND
I LOVE YOU
To: my friend

Winter Concept Check

Directions: Use this concept check to see how well your children remember the concepts they've learned in the last few months. Give each child a copy of the following page. Then, have the children listen carefully and follow your directions.

1. Give the bear standing in front of the snow fort a red hat.
2. Draw hats on the three bears skating together. Make two hats the same and one hat different.
3. Draw a red bird in the center of the widest tree.
4. Color the medium-sized snowball green.
5. Draw three blue snowflakes on the narrowest tree. Make one small, the next one smaller, and the last one the smallest.
6. Find the bear standing behind the snow fort. Color his scarf purple.
7. Give the first skating bear a red coat. Skip a bear and give the next bear a blue coat.
8. Color the skates of the third bear in line orange.
9. Draw a blue snowflake above the skating bear nearest the tree on the left.
10. Draw a crack in the ice below the bear that fell.
11. Draw a purple snowflake in one corner of your paper.
12. Color the trunk of the tree on the left brown.
13. Give the middle skating bear a black coat.
14. Use a black crayon to draw a snowman on the right side of the snow fort.
15. Color many of the snowflakes blue.
16. Color the big snowball black.
17. Give the second skating bear a yellow scarf.
18. Draw a brown nest in the tree farthest from the snow fort.
19. Give a few bears brown ears.
20. Find one bear with no scarf. Give him a blue scarf.
21. Give the last bear in line yellow mittens.

You deserve a fun day in the snow for all your hard work!

Name ______________________

Brennan's Gold Coins

Directions: Gather enough coins so each child can have three. (Pennies will work fine.) Then, encourage the children to listen carefully as you read the story below. As you read the story, have the children line up their coins in a row or mix them up, depending on the story line. Remind the children to listen for the word *row*. After you read the story, ask the children the questions listed on the next page.

Brennan loved his Grandpa O'Grady very much. Grandpa O'Grady was from Ireland and he liked to tell Brennan stories about leprechauns, rainbows, and pots of gold coins. One St. Patrick's Day, Grandpa O'Grady told this story to Brennan.

"Once upon a time there was a wee lad bear just like yourself. He worked very hard for his grandpappy — chopping wood and weeding the potato garden. His grandpappy gave him three gold coins for his hard work."

"The wee bear was very proud of his gold coins. He jingled them in his pocket, he flipped them into the air, he twirled them on the table, and he shined them so they were very bright. Just before bedtime, the wee bear put his three gold coins in a row on his nightstand. (Help the children line up their coins so they're in a row.) Then, he went to sleep."

"When the wee bear woke up the next morning, he looked over at his nightstand. What do you think he saw? His gold coins weren't in a row anymore. They were all jumbled up. (Help the children mix up their coins so they aren't in a row anymore.)"

"'Well,' thought the wee bear, 'I must have bumped my nightstand in the night and jumbled up my coins.'"

"The next night, the wee bear put his coins in a row again, just like the night before. (Help the children line up their coins in a row.)"

"When the wee bear woke up the next morning, the coins weren't in a row. They were all jumbled up again. (Have the children mix up their coins.)"

"Now, the wee bear wasn't sure what to think. 'Maybe it was my cat,' he thought. So, that night he put his coins in a row again. (Have the children line up their coins in a row.) Then, he put his cat outside for the night."

"When the wee bear woke up the next morning, what do you think he found? Were the coins in a row? No, sir! They were all jumbled up, just like the two times before. (Have the children mix up their coins.)"

"The wee lad bear was very confused. The cat couldn't have moved the coins and he hadn't bumped the nightstand. Who could have moved the coins?"

March

Brennan's Gold Coins, continued

"The wee lad bear went to his grandpappy and told him about the strange happenings. His grandpappy just smiled and said, 'Lad, those are magic coins some leprechauns gave me. Leprechauns are such silly little people — they love to play tricks. It was the leprechauns who jumbled up your gold coins.'"

"Then, Grandpappy took the wee bear on his knee and said, 'Never spend those gold coins. They will bring you lots of good luck as long as you have them!'"

Brennan looked at his Grandpa O'Grady. "Was that a true story, Grandpa?" asked Brennan.

Grandpa O'Grady reached down deep into his pocket and pulled out three gold coins. Brennan's eyes grew very big. "I was that wee lad bear," said Grandpa O'Grady. "It was my grandpappy who gave me the coins. I want to give the coins to you now, Brennan."

Brennan was very excited! He could hardly wait to put the gold coins in a row by his bed that night!

Questions:

1. What did Grandpa O'Grady like to tell stories about?
2. Why did the wee bear in the story get three gold coins?
3. What did the wee bear do with his coins each night when he went to bed?
4. Tell what the coins looked like each morning when the wee bear woke up.
5. What did the wee bear think jumbled up the coins?
6. What did the wee bear's grandpappy say jumbled up the coins?
7. Who was the wee bear in the story?
8. What size is a wee bear?
9. Show how we lined up our coins in a row.
10. Do you think it would be fun to have magic coins? What would you do with them?

Lions, Lambs, and Bears: Instructions

Give each child a copy of *Lions, Lambs, and Bears*. Have the children listen carefully and follow your directions. Remind them to listen for the word *row*.

1. Draw three green buttons in a row on the bear on the right.
2. Draw three red birds that aren't in a row, under the sun.
3. Color the four animals in a row brown.
4. Draw a row of blue clouds in the sky.
5. If both lambs are in a row, give each one a yellow hat. If both lambs aren't in a row, give each one an orange hat.
6. Draw three yellow butterflies that aren't in a row.
7. Draw a row of three purple flowers next to the brown lamb.
8. Draw three green frogs in a row at the bottom of your paper.
9. If the bears are in a row, draw a smiley face on the sun. If the bears aren't in a row, draw a sad face on the sun.
10. Draw a row of three black ants next to the white lamb.
11. If the lion is in a row, color its face black. If the lion isn't in a row, color its face brown.
12. Draw some bees below the row of clouds.
13. Draw three red butterflies in a row.
14. If the kites are in a row, color the middle kite green. If the kites aren't in a row, color the middle kite orange.
15. Draw a yellow bunny by the row of flowers.

What a beautiful day for these animals to play outside!

Lions, Lambs, and Bears

Name ____________________

March: *row*

Something Green

Directions: Give a copy of *Color It Green* to each child. Have the children color all the pictures green and cut them out. Then, encourage the children to listen carefully as you read the story below. Have the children hold up their pictures when you talk about them in the story. After you read the story, ask the children the questions listed on the next page.

St. Patrick's Day was getting near. Brennan and all his friends were planning a parade. Brennan's friend Bert wanted to be in the parade, but he didn't know what to wear. Brennan said, "Just make sure you wear something green on your head!"

Bert thought it would be easy to find something green to wear. He could hardly wait to march in the parade! He raced home and decided he'd better think of something green to wear on his head. "I know what to wear. I'll wear a pine tree. It's green." Bert put a pine tree on his head and went to show Brennan.

"You can't wear that," said Brennan. "It's too prickly. You'd better find some other green thing to wear."

Bert went back home. "I can't wear a pine tree, so what other green thing can I wear? I know! I'll wear a frog." He put a frog on his head and went to show Brennan.

"You can't wear a frog on your head," said Brennan. "It will hop away. You'll have to find some other green thing to wear."

Bert went back home. "I can't wear a pine tree or a frog. What other green thing can I wear? I know! I'll wear a turtle." He put a turtle on his head and went to show Brennan.

Brennan said, "You can't wear a turtle on your head. It will wiggle off. You'll have to find some other green thing to wear."

Bert went back home. "I can't wear a pine tree, a frog, or a turtle. What other green thing can I wear? I know! I'll wear a cucumber." He quickly found a cucumber in his garden and put it on his head. Then, he ran to show Brennan.

Brennan said, "You can't wear a cucumber. It will slide off your head. You'll have to find some other green thing to wear."

At home, Bert thought again. "I can't wear a pine tree, a frog, a turtle, or a cucumber. What other green thing can I wear? I've got it! I'll wear a snake." Bert found a snake and put it on his head. He went to show Brennan again.

When Brennan saw the snake, he said, "Oh, no, Bert. You can't wear a snake. It might bite you!"

Something Green, continued

Bert went home again. He thought, "I can't wear a pine tree, a frog, a turtle, a cucumber, or a snake. What other green thing can I wear? I know. I'll wear olives!"

When Bert showed Brennan the olives, Brennan said, "Bert, you can't wear olives. They will roll off your head. You'll have to find some other green thing to wear."

Bert went home again. "Gee," he said, "I can't wear a pine tree, a frog, a turtle, a cucumber, a snake, or olives. What other green thing can I wear? I know, I'll wear a leaf. It will be perfect and I'll be able to be in the parade." He put a leaf on his head and went to show Brennan.

When Brennan saw Bert, he said, "You can't wear a leaf, Bert. It will blow away."

"Well," said Bert. "I guess I can't be in the parade. I can't think of anything green to wear on my head. A pine tree is too prickly, a frog will hop away, a turtle will wiggle off my head, a cucumber will slide off my head, a snake might bite me, olives will roll off my head, and a leaf will blow away. I sure wish I could think of something green to wear on my head."

"Bert, you've tried very hard to find something green to wear in the parade," said Brennan. "I know you really want to be in the parade, so I've got something for you." He handed Bert a green hat. It fit perfectly!

"Thank you, Brennan," said Bert. "Now, I can be in the parade!"

Questions:

1. What holiday was getting near?
2. What did Bert have to do to be in the parade?
3. One thing Bert tried to wear was a pine tree. What were some of the other things he tried to wear?
4. Tell why Brennan said Bert couldn't wear a frog in the parade.
5. Why couldn't Bert wear a leaf in the parade?
6. Why did Brennan give Bert a green hat?
7. What are some other green things Bert could have tried to wear?
8. What color might you have to wear for a Valentine's Day parade?
9. Would you rather march in a parade or watch a parade? Explain your answer.
10. What are parades for?

Color It Green

Name ___________________________

St. Patrick's Day: Instructions

Give each child a copy of *St. Patrick's Day*. Have the children listen carefully and follow your directions. Remind them to listen for the word *other*.

Look at the rainbows.

1. Color three of the rainbows red and blue.
2. Color the other rainbow purple and orange.

Look at the bears.

1. Draw a red beard on one bear.
2. Draw orange beards on the other bears.

Look at the shamrocks.

1. Color two shamrocks green.
2. Color the other shamrock brown.

Look at the coins.

1. Color three of the coins yellow.
2. Color the other coins blue.
3. Give one yellow coin a sad face.
4. Give the other yellow coins happy faces.

Look at the pots.

1. Color one pot black.
2. Color the other pots brown.

Look at the hats.

1. Give two hats purple buckles.
2. Give the other hats yellow buckles.
3. Color the hats with purple buckles brown.
4. Color the other hats green.

St. Patrick's Day is a fun holiday, isn't it?

St. Patrick's Day

Name ______________________

Kite Trouble

Directions: Encourage the children to listen carefully as you read the story below. After you read the story, ask the children the questions listed at the bottom of the page.

It was a warm, windy day in March. Brennan thought it was good weather to fly a kite. He had a brand new kite he wanted to fly. It was purple with a big, pretty butterfly on it.

Brennan took his kite outside. He started to run with the kite as fast as he could. It went up into the air for a few seconds, then suddenly came crashing to the ground. Oh, that made Brennan sad. His brand new kite was ruined.

The next day, Brennan's dad bought a new kite for him. He told Brennan that maybe this kite would fly better. It was green with a huge black spider in the center of it. Brennan took his new kite outside. It went up into the air very easily and stayed there for a few minutes. Then, it started to swoop down, and the next thing he knew — it was caught in a tree.

Brennan climbed the tree to get the kite down. When he reached the kite, he could see that it was ruined. Brennan was very sad. His first kite wouldn't fly and neither would his next kite.

Again, Brennan's dad bought a new kite for him. This one was red with a large ice cream cone on it. Brennan took it outside. It went high up into the air. After a few minutes, Brennan thought that this kite was a good flier. Then, the kite started to swoop just like the others had. It landed in the neighbor's pond. The kite was ruined!

Brennan said, "My first kite crashed, my next kite got tangled up in a tree, and my last kite landed in a pond. I think I'll give up kite flying. March might be good weather for flying kites, but it's also good weather for riding bikes."

So, Brennan hopped on his bike and went for a long ride. "What good weather for riding bikes!" he thought.

Questions:

1. What was the weather like?
2. Tell what Brennan's first kite looked like.
3. What did Brennan's next kite look like?
4. Tell what Brennan's last kite looked like.
5. What happened the first time Brennan tried to fly a kite?
6. Tell what happened the next time Brennan tried to fly a kite.
7. What happened the last time Brennan tried to fly a kite?
8. What did Brennan decide to do at the end of the story?
9. Name some other things you can play with outside.
10. If you could make your own design on a kite, what would it look like?

Kites for Everyone: Instructions

Give each child a copy of *Kites for Everyone*. Have the children listen carefully and follow your directions. Remind them to listen for the words *first*, *next*, and *last*. Also, tell the children to count from the left. (The first kite is the one farthest to the left, the second kite is second from the left, etc.)

Use your crayons to color the kites.

1. Color the first kite red and black.
2. Color the next kite green and blue.
3. Color the last kite purple and yellow.
4. Color the third kite blue and orange.
5. Color the next kite orange and green.
6. Color the fifth kite yellow and red.

Let's find out who these kites belong to. Use your pencil for this part.

1. Draw a line from the third kite to the girl bear.
2. Draw a line from the first kite to the bear who's ready to play baseball.
3. Draw a line from the next kite to the bear with a butterfly on his head.
4. Draw a line from the fourth kite to the bear with a bird.
5. Draw a line from the next kite to the bear wearing shorts.
6. Draw yourself beside the first bear. Draw a line from the last kite to you.

You're flying a kite with the best of the bears!

Kites for Everyone

Name ______________________

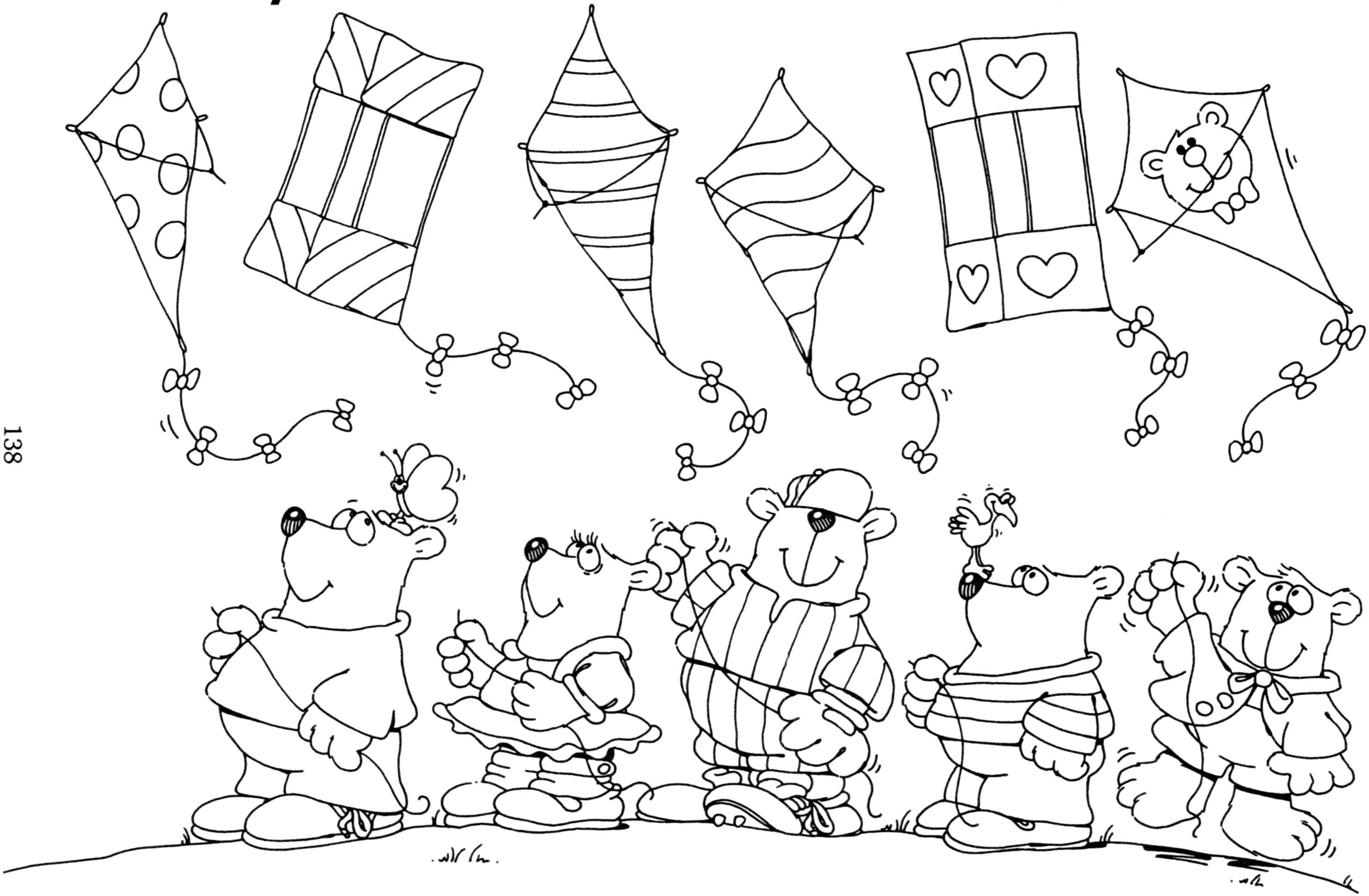

Before and *After* Questions

Directions: Ask the children the following questions. Ask them to listen carefully for the words *before* and *after*. When you're done, have the children make up *before* and *after* questions for each other.

1. What do you do before you go to bed?
2. What do you do before you go outside on a snowy day?
3. What do you do after you get home from school?
4. How do you feel after you go to a circus?
5. What do you put on after your socks?
6. What should you do before you eat supper?
7. What do you do after you spill a glass of milk?
8. How do you look after you get a haircut?
9. What do you do before you go swimming?
10. What do you do before you go down a slide?
11. What should you do after you cut your finger?
12. What do you say after someone says "Hi"?
13. How would you feel after running in a race?
14. What do you do before you drink a glass of orange juice?
15. What do you do before you draw a picture?
16. What do you do after your mom lights all the candles on your birthday cake?
17. What do you do before you go to school?
18. What happens before there's a rainbow?
19. What happens after you jump off a diving board?
20. What should you do before you cross a street?

Note: These questions may have more than one correct answer.

Before and After Spring

Directions: Give each child a copy of *Outdoor Fun with Brennan*. Tell the children you're going to read a story about Brennan playing outside before and after spring. Encourage them to listen carefully as you read the story.

When you're done reading the story, ask the children the questions listed at the bottom of the page. Then, the children can finish their pictures so they show what Brennan did before and after spring.

Brennan liked to play outside during different times of the year. He could always find something fun to do, no matter what season it was. Before spring, it was usually very cold outside — it was winter. When Brennan went out to play, he wore his hat, mittens, a big coat, and a scarf. All of these clothes kept Brennan warm while he played in the snow.

One of Brennan's favorite things to do before spring came was to build snowmen. He especially liked to build large snowmen that were made of three or four heavy snowballs. One day, Brennan rolled the balls of snow until they were so heavy he could hardly push them any more. Then, he got a friend to help him stack up the snowballs on top of each other. When the snowballs were all in place, he gave the snowman eyes made of carrots and a mouth and nose made of small rocks. There was only one thing left to do — give the snowman a tall, black hat. There, his snowman was finished!

After the snowman was finished, Brennan rode his red sled down the steepest hills he could find. Whee! He really liked to play outside before spring came.

After many weeks, the weather began to change. It wasn't winter any more — it was spring. After spring came, Brennan was ready to play outside again. He put on his baseball cap and glove and ran outside into the spring air. He saw two yellow flowers growing near his house. Brennan thought they looked very pretty.

After Brennan looked at the flowers, he pulled his red wagon out of the shed. He hadn't played with his wagon since last fall. Brennan put his glove into the wagon and began to pull it to the baseball field. He was glad it was spring.

Questions:

1. When was the weather cold?
2. Tell what Brennan wore outside in the winter.
3. What was one of Brennan's favorite things to do before spring came?
4. Why did Brennan need someone to help him build his snowman?
5. Tell what the snowman looked like when Brennan was done making him.
6. How did the weather change?
7. What did Brennan do after spring came?
8. Where did Brennan find his red wagon?
9. What is your favorite season? Why?
10. What season comes after spring?

Outdoor Fun with Brennan

Name ____________________

March: *before, after*

Brennan Goes to the Grocery Store

Directions: Encourage the children to listen carefully as you read the story below. Remind the children to listen for the word *several*. After you read the story, ask the children the questions listed at the bottom of the page.

Brennan's mom always fixed healthy meals for their family. Brennan liked to go to the grocery store to get the food she needed. His mom helped Brennan by dividing the shopping list into the four food groups — fruits and vegetables, milk and cheese, meat and fish, and breads and cereals. Brennan was all ready to go the grocery store.

When Brennan got to the grocery store, he wheeled his cart into the fruits and vegetables section. He needed some vegetables for a salad. He needed lettuce, a pepper, and several tomatoes. He picked up two tomatoes, but that wasn't enough. He put a few more into his cart. There, that made several tomatoes.

Next, he had to pick up several apples for a fruit salad. One, two, three, four apples — that made several apples. He also picked out one banana and one pineapple for the fruit salad.

The next section was the dairy section. Brennan knew he could find milk and cheese here. He needed one gallon of milk and several kinds of cheese. He picked out one, two, three, four...several kinds of cheese. He put the milk and cheese in his cart. He also got some chocolate ice cream for dessert.

The third section he went to was the meat and fish section. He had to buy several chicken drumsticks. He picked out three or four that looked delicious. Oops, he almost forgot the hamburger for tomorrow's supper!

The last section Brennan went to was the breads and cereals section. His mom had asked him to get one loaf of wheat bread and several rolls. He also got to pick out a box of his favorite cereal.

Brennan took his cart to the checkout counter and paid the cashier with the money his mom had given him. "Boy," said the cashier. "Your family sure eats healthy foods — something from every food group!"

Questions:

1. What kind of meals did Brennan's mom fix?
2. How did Brennan's mom divide up the shopping list?
3. What are the four food groups?
4. What did Brennan get in the fruits and vegetables section?
5. Tell what Brennan got in the milk and cheese section.
6. What did Brennan get in the meat and fish section?
7. Tell what Brennan got in the breads and cereals section.
8. Who did Brennan pay for the groceries?
9. Name some other foods in the fruits and vegetables food group.
10. Which food group has yogurt, cottage cheese, and butter?

Fill 'Em Up: Instructions

Give each child a copy of *Fill 'Em Up*. Have the children listen carefully and follow your directions. Remind them to listen for the word *several*. Encourage the children to draw small foods inside the bags so there is enough room to draw everything you say to draw.

Look at section one.

1. Draw two red apples inside the top bag and one inside the bottom bag.
2. Draw an orange inside the top bag.
3. Draw two ears of corn inside the top bag and one inside the bottom bag.
4. Circle the bag with several kinds of fruits and vegetables with your green crayon.

Look at section two.

1. Draw three cartons of milk inside the bottom bag with your orange crayon.
2. Draw one yellow piece of cheese inside the bottom bag and several pieces of cheese inside the top bag.
3. Draw one red carton of ice cream inside each bag.
4. Circle the bag with several cartons of milk with your red crayon.

Look at section three.

1. Draw two brown hamburgers inside the top bag.
2. Draw one red hot dog inside the bottom bag and one inside the top bag.
3. Draw two orange pieces of fish inside the top bag.
4. Circle the bag with several kinds of meat and fish with your blue crayon.

Look at section four.

1. Draw three blue boxes of cereal inside the bottom bag and one inside the top bag.
2. Draw one brown loaf of bread inside the top bag.
3. Draw several yellow rolls inside the bottom bag.
4. Circle the bag with several boxes of cereal with your yellow crayon.

Now, draw a picture of your favorite dessert in the middle of the page. Yum!

Fill 'Em Up

Name ______________________

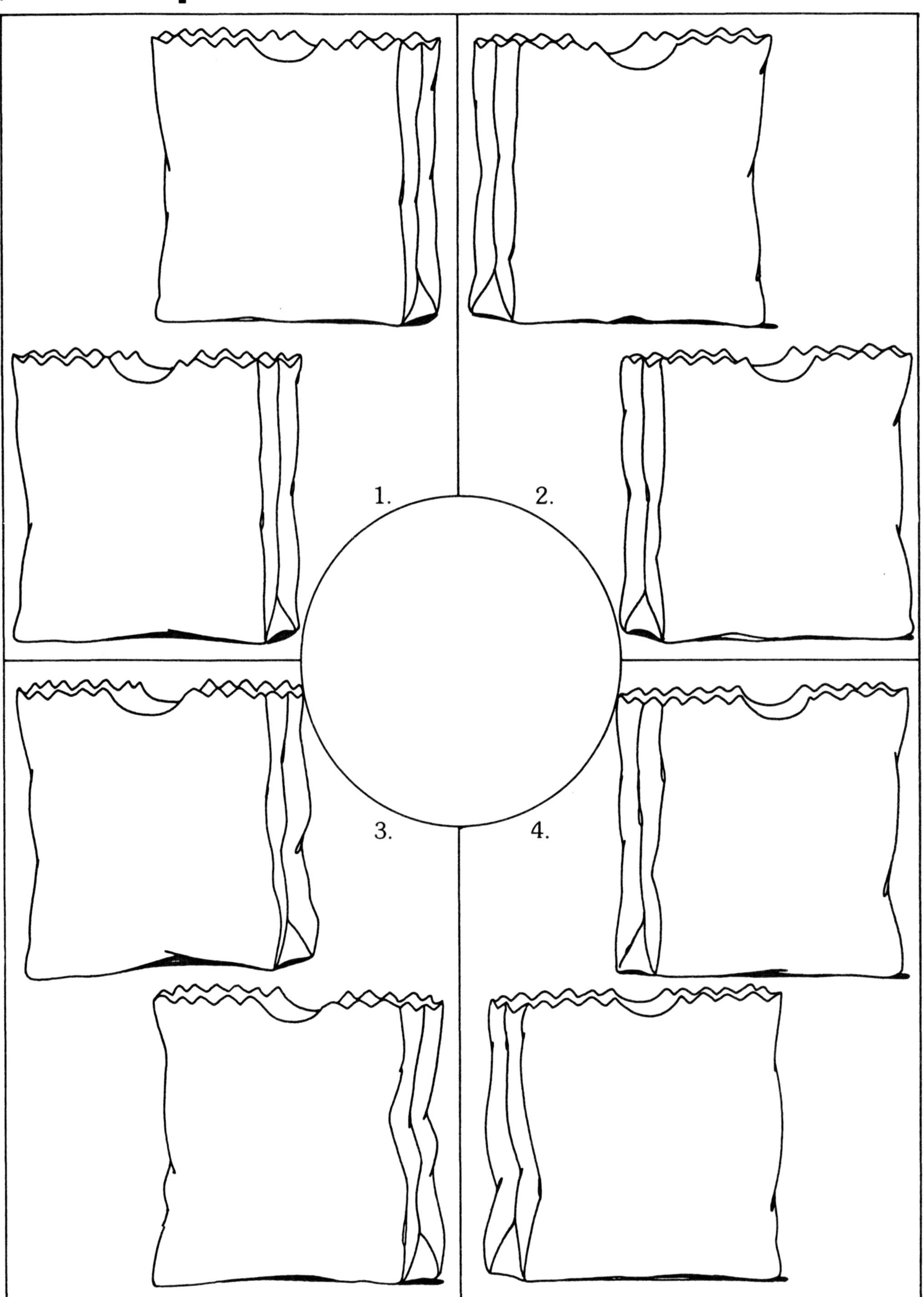

Home Lesson

Dear ______________,

During the month of March, we have been working on these concepts: *row*, *other*, *first*, *next*, *last*, *before*, *after*, and *several*. You can help your child review these concepts by giving your child the sheet attached to this page. Read the directions below and encourage your child to listen carefully and follow your directions. Here are the materials you will need: a box of eight crayons, a table, a chair, and a quiet place to work.

Directions:

Look at row one.

1. Put a green X on the pictures of pots before they're filled with coins.
2. Draw a black circle around the pictures of pots after they're filled with coins.
3. Draw several yellow coins in an empty pot.

Look at row two.

1. Color the first lion and lamb yellow.
2. Color the next lion and lamb blue.
3. Color the last lion and lamb red.

Look at row three.

1. Find the picture of the bear after he shaved his beard. Color the bear's hat purple.
2. Find the picture of the bear before he shaved his beard. Color the bear's hat orange.

Look at row four.

1. If the kites are in a row, color their tails purple. If the kites aren't in a row, color their tails black.
2. Color the first kite on the left yellow and the last kite on the right brown.
3. Color the other kites blue.
4. Circle several kites with your red crayon.

Look at row five.

1. Color the first coin on the left brown.
2. Color the next coin yellow.
3. Put a red X on the other coins.

Have a Happy Spring!

Sincerely,

____

Name ______________________

1.

2.

3.

4.

5.

Easter Eggs for Everyone

Directions: Give each child three copies of *Color the Eggs* (one page for each animal in the story). As you read the story below, have the children color the appropriate number of eggs the right color for each animal. When you're done, ask the children the questions listed at the bottom of the page.

Brennan Bear was getting ready for Easter, making Easter baskets for his friends. He put Easter grass in the baskets, then added jelly beans, marshmallow chicks, and a chocolate bunny. "Oops!" he said. "I almost forgot the Easter eggs. But, I don't know what color eggs my friends like. I think I'll go ask them."

First, Brennan went to see Todd Turtle. "What color Easter eggs would you like in your Easter basket?" asked Brennan.

"Well, I like all colors, but I really like my green shell. Could you color some, but not many of my eggs green?" asked Todd.

"Certainly!" answered Brennan.

Next, Brennan visited Hubert Horse. "What color would you like your Easter eggs to be?" asked Brennan.

Hubert answered, "Well, I like all colors, but I really like to eat red apples. Could you make some, but not many of my eggs red?"

"Certainly!" answered Brennan.

Last, he went to see Barry Bird. "What color would you like your Easter eggs to be?" asked Brennan.

Barry said, "I like all colors, but I'm really proud of my blue feathers. Could you color some, but not many of my eggs blue?"

"Certainly!" said Brennan.

Finally, Brennan was ready to color the eggs. He want back home. Oh, no! Brennan forgot to write down the colors everyone wanted. He couldn't remember any of the colors. Could you help Brennan?

April

Questions:

1. What holiday was Brennan getting ready for?
2. Name the things Brennan put in the Easter baskets.
3. What color eggs did Todd Turtle choose?
4. How many eggs did Todd want of his favorite color?
5. What color eggs did Hubert Horse choose?
6. How many eggs did Hubert want of his favorite color?
7. What color eggs did Barry Bird choose?
8. How many eggs did Barry want of his favorite color?
9. What color would you like your Easter eggs to be? Why?
10. What are some other things you might find in an Easter basket?

Color the Eggs

Name ______________________

Spring Weather: Instructions

Give each child a copy of *Spring Weather*. Have the children listen carefully and follow your directions. Remind them to listen for the words *some* and *not many*.

1. Color some, but not many of the buds on the tree green.
2. Give the bear with some, but not many flowers a red shirt with blue buttons.
3. Color some, but not many yellow polka dots on the sleeping bear's blanket.
4. Give some, but not many of the bears brown ears.
5. Give the bear with some, but not many balloons a purple dress.
6. Color some, but not many sections of the parachute purple.
7. Look at the bear with many flowers. Color some, but not many of the flowers blue.
8. Color the basket with some, but not many eggs brown.
9. Draw some, but not many orange eggs beside the sitting bear.
10. Look at the basket with many eggs. Color some, but not many of the eggs red.
11. Color some, but not many stripes on the old bear's shirt.
12. Give some, but not many of the bears black shoes.
13. Look at the bear with many balloons. Color some, but not many of the balloons purple.
14. Draw some, but not many bluebirds in the sky.
15. Give some, but not many of the bears brown faces.

What a beautiful spring day!

Spring Weather

Name ______________________

April: *some, not many*

Easter Egg Hunt

Directions: Encourage the children to listen carefully as you read the story below. After you read the story, ask the children the questions listed at the bottom of the page.

Brennan was very excited. He had invited some of his friends over for an Easter egg hunt. He got four Easter baskets ready and dyed twenty Easter eggs. His dad helped him hide the eggs in the nearby woods. Just as they finished hiding the eggs, Max Mouse, Sam Squirrel, Kari Cat, and Hanna Hen showed up. They were very excited because they loved to hunt for eggs. Plus, Brennan was giving a prize to the one who found the most eggs — a chocolate bunny!

Brennan gave each friend a basket and shouted "Go!" Everyone ran into the woods and began to look under rocks, in trees, and behind stumps for the hidden eggs. Brennan could hear them laughing and shouting as they found the eggs, one by one.

After a while, everyone came back. Max Mouse came back first, carrying an empty basket. "What happened?" asked Brennan. "Why don't you have any eggs?" "Well," sniffled Max. "I'm too little. I couldn't lift the eggs into my basket. That's why it's empty."

Sam Squirrel arrived next. His basket was so full he could hardly lift it. "Wow!" exclaimed Brennan. "How did you find so many eggs?" Sam smiled. "I'm good at finding things. After all, I have to find nuts all the time!"

Kari Cat came in next. She didn't have as many eggs as Sam, but her basket was almost full. She was a good hunter, but she had spent most of her time playing with the eggs, batting them back and forth with her paws!

"Where's Hanna Hen?" asked Brennan. Everyone looked around and saw her sitting in her basket. "How many eggs did you find?" asked Brennan. "Just one," said Hanna with a secret smile. "Then, your basket is almost empty," said Brennan. "Is that why you're sitting in it?" "No," replied Hanna.

All of a sudden, they heard a crackling noise. Hanna stepped out of the basket and everyone gasped. There was a baby chick in the basket! It had come just in time for Easter.

Questions:

1. Tell how many baskets Brennan got ready.
2. How many eggs did Brennan dye?
3. Who helped Brennan hide the eggs?
4. Who came to the Easter egg hunt?
5. What was the prize for finding the most eggs?
6. Was Max Mouse's basket empty or full? Why?
7. Was Sam Squirrel's basket empty or full? Why?
8. What did Kari Cat like to do with her eggs?
9. How many eggs did Hanna Hen get?
10. What was Hanna's secret?

Easter Bunny: Instructions

Give each child a copy of *Easter Bunny*. Have the children listen carefully and follow your directions. Remind them to listen for the words *almost*, *empty*, and *full*.

Look at the jars of jelly beans.

1. Color the jar that's almost full yellow.
2. Put a purple X on the jar that's almost empty.
3. Color the empty jar green.

Look at the Easter baskets.

1. Find the basket that's full. Color almost all the eggs red.
2. Find the basket that's almost empty. Color it brown.

Look at the vases.

1. Draw a red circle around the vase that's almost empty.
2. Color the vase that's full blue.
3. Color the flowers in the vase that's almost full purple.
4. Put a black X on the empty vase.

Find the eggs on the top shelf.

1. Color the chick that's almost hatched purple.
2. Color the chick that's hatched yellow.

Find the bags of candy.

1. Color the candy in the bag that's almost empty green.
2. Find the bag that's almost full. Color almost all the candy orange.

Find the Easter egg dye.

1. Draw a green circle around the jar that's almost full.
2. Put a blue X on the jar that's almost empty.

What's your favorite thing about Easter?

Easter Bunny

Name ______________________

April: *almost, empty, full*

Brennan's Friends Visit

Directions: Make a set of paper bears, following the directions on the next page. Then, draw a picture of a house on the chalkboard, according to the directions on the next page.

Next, tell the children you're going to read a story about Brennan and his friends. You'll be sticking the bears on the chalkboard as you read the story, so make sure you have some tape to stick to the back of the bears. When you're done reading the story, ask the children the questions listed at the bottom of the page.

It was a Saturday morning. After Brennan watched all of his favorite cartoons, he asked his mom if he could have four of his friends over to play. She said he could if everyone played nicely together. Brennan said that they would, so he quickly called four of his friends and they came over to his house. (Unfold the bears and show the children all five of them.)

Brennan and his friends played nicely together in the family room. (Put the bears on the chalkboard in the bottom room.)

After a while, Brennan and two of his friends started to fight with each other. Brennan's mom told them they weren't being nice, and then she separated them. She put Brennan in one bedroom, one of his friends in another room, and the other bear in another room. They were separated. (Cut each of three bears off the chain and put them in the top three rooms of the house.)

The other two bears were being good, so they could stay together and play. A few minutes later, Brennan's mom went to check on the three bears who had been fighting. She asked them if they were ready to play nicely. They promised not to fight anymore, so they were allowed back together with the other two bears. (Put the three bears in the same room as the other two bears.)

Brennan told his friends, "It's much nicer to be together with your friends than to be separated from them!"

All of Brennan's friends agreed, so they played nicely the rest of the day.

Questions:

1. What did Brennan do before he asked if his friends could come over?
2. How many friends came over to Brennan's house?
3. Where did all the bears play first?
4. Who started fighting?
5. Tell what Brennan's mom did when three of the bears started fighting.
6. Why do you think Brennan liked being together with his friends?
7. How many bears were there altogether in this story?
8. What does it mean to be separated?
9. Tell what you like to do when you're together with your friends.
10. Make up four names for Brennan's friends.

Brennan's Friends Visit, continued

Directions: Make a chain of paper bears by following these steps:

1. Cut a brown piece of paper so it measures 4" by 15".
2. Fold the paper like a fan so you have ten total sides, each measuring 1" by 4".
3. Trace the bear pattern below onto the appropriate outside section of the fan. Make sure you draw the pattern on the paper so that the center of the bear's body runs along the side with five folds.

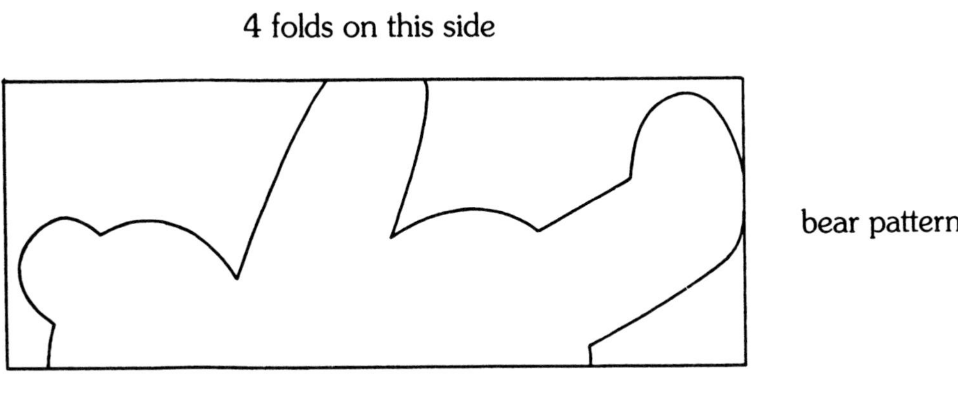

Now, draw a large picture of the house below on the chalkboard. You'll be putting the bears in the rooms of the house, so gather some tape or something sticky to hold the bears in the rooms.

When you're done, read *Brennan's Friends Visit*, using the bears and the picture of the house to help tell the story.

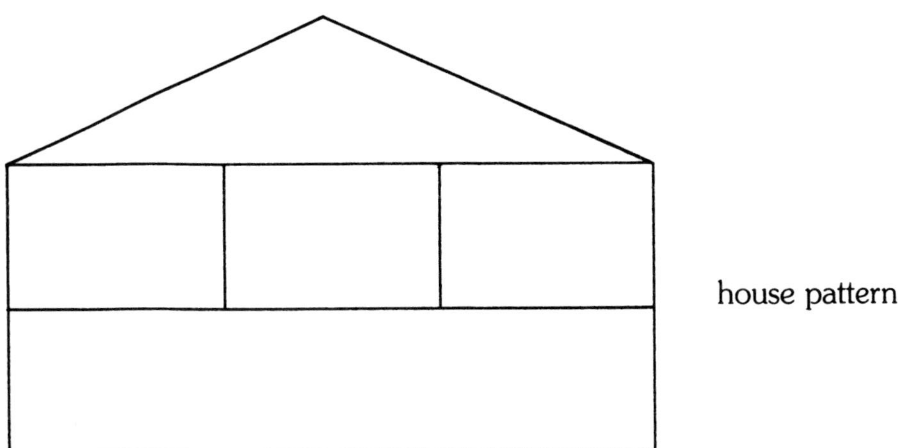

Fun in the Park: Instructions

Give each child a copy of *Fun in the Park*. Have the children listen carefully and follow your directions. Remind them to listen for the words *together* and *separated*.

1. Find the bears who are roller skating together. Color their skates orange.
2. Color the jogging bear who's separated from the others brown.
3. Color the clouds that are together yellow.
4. Find the bears who are separated by a park bench. Color their skates blue.
5. Draw a green circle around the trees that are together.
6. Find the bears who are jogging together. Color their clothes red and yellow.
7. Draw a purple circle around the sitting bear who's separated from the others.
8. Color the three flowers that are together blue.
9. Find the three clouds that are separated. Color each cloud a different color.
10. Find the bears who are roller skating together. Color their pants brown.
11. Find the flower that's separated from the other flowers. Color it purple.
12. Find the bears who are sitting together. Color their clothes green and yellow.
13. Find the bears who are jogging together. Color their ears red.
14. Find the roller skating bears who have been separated. Put a black X on each bear.
15. Find the flowers that are together by the joggers. Color the flowers orange.

What's your favorite thing to do in the park?

Fun in the Park

Name ______________________

April: *together, separated*

Eggs-actly the Same

Directions: Draw the four eggs below on the chalkboard, numbering them from 1 to 4. Then, draw four blank eggs beside them.

1. 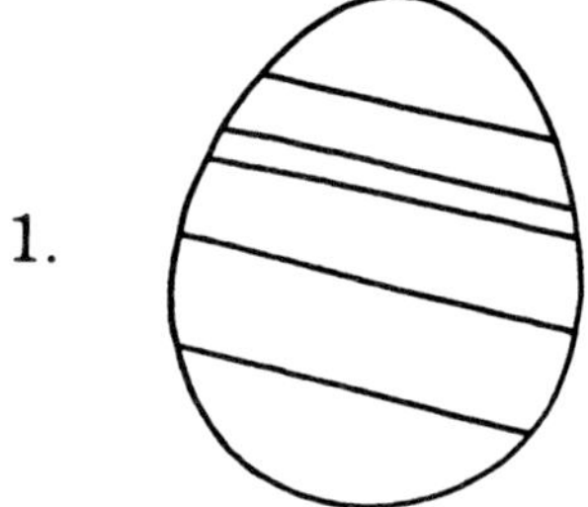

2. 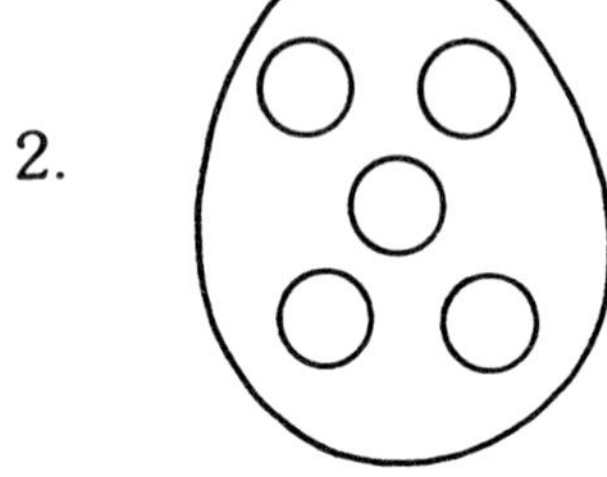

3. 

4. 

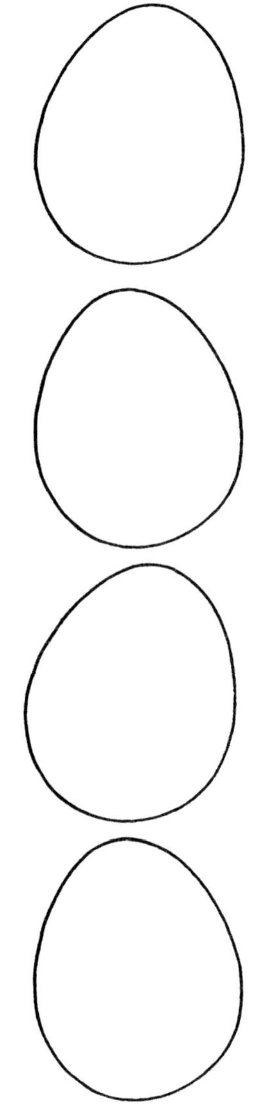

Now, have the children take turns decorating the blanks eggs, following the directions below. The children should decorate the blank egg beside the numbered egg in the directions.

1. Put as many stripes on the blank egg as are on egg number 1.
2. Draw an equal number of circles on the blank egg as are on egg number two.
3. Make the blank egg match egg number 3.
4. Make the blank egg the same as egg number 4.

You decorated the eggs very well!

Beary Merry Bears: Instructions

Give each child a copy of *Beary Merry Bears*. Have the children listen carefully and follow your directions. Remind them to listen for the words *equal*, *same*, *as many*, and *match*.

Look at row one.

1. Draw a blue circle around the group of bears that matches the group in the box.
2. Put a red X on the group of bears that doesn't match the bears in the box.

Look at row two.

1. Put a green X on the bears that don't look the same as the one in the box.
2. Draw a yellow circle around the bear that looks the same as the one in the box.

Look at row three.

1. Draw an orange circle around the bear who has as many balloons as the bear in the box.
2. Put a brown X on the bears who don't have as many balloons as the bear in the box.

Look at row four.

1. Put a purple X on the bears whose flags aren't the same as the bear in the box.
2. Draw a black circle around the bear whose flag is the same as the bear in the box.

Look at row five.

1. Draw a red circle around the bear who has a number of balls equal to the bear in the box.
2. Put a yellow X on the bears who don't have a number of balls equal to the bear in the box.

These merry bears should be in a circus!

Beary Merry Bears

Name ______________________

1.

2.

3.

4.

5.

Home Lesson

Dear ________________,

During the month of April, we have been working on these concepts: *some*, *not many*, *almost*, *empty*, *full*, *together*, *separated*, *equal*, *same*, *as many*, and *match*. You can help your child review these concepts by giving your child the sheet attached to this page. Read the directions below and encourage your child to listen carefully and follow your directions. Here are the materials you will need: a box of eight crayons, a table, a chair, and a quiet place to work.

Directions:

1. Find egg one. Color almost all of the circles purple. Color the rest yellow.
2. Find egg two. Color some, but not many of the apples red.
3. Find egg three. Color the bunnies that are the same brown.
4. Find egg four. Draw a green circle around the ducks that are together. Put a yellow X on the duck that's separated from the others.
5. Find egg five. Color the basket that's full of eggs black. Color the basket that's almost empty brown.
6. Find egg six. Color the umbrellas so they match the color of most of the circles in egg one.
7. Find egg seven. Draw as many apples in this egg as there are in egg two.
8. Find egg eight. Draw an equal number of flowers in this egg as there are in egg nine.

Have a sunny day!

Sincerely,

____

Name ______________________________

Pair Up!

Directions: Discuss the meaning of the word *pair*. Ask the children to name some clothes they're wearing that come in pairs. Then, have them name pairs of things in the room. When the children understand the concept of *pair*, tell them you're going to play a guessing game. Encourage the children to listen carefully as you ask questions about different pairs of things.

1. What pair do you wear on your legs?
2. What pair do you wear on your feet?
3. What pair do you clap with?
4. What pair do you put on your feet before you put on your shoes?
5. What pair do you put on your face to help you see better?
6. What pair do you wear on your hands when it's cold?
7. What pair do you cut with?
8. What pair do you wear on your feet when it's snowing?
9. What pair do birds fly with?
10. What do we call a pair of family members who were born on the same day?

What would you like to have a pair of?

Dress-a-Bear: Instructions

Give each child a copy of *Dress-a-Bear*. Have the children listen carefully and follow your directions. Remind the children to listen for the word *pair*.

1. Draw a pair of blue pants on the bear.
2. Give the bear a red shirt and a pair of yellow mittens.
3. Draw a pair of blue clouds in the sky.
4. Draw a pair of orange flowers beside the bear.
5. Draw a pair of green glasses on the bear.
6. Draw a pair of purple buttons on the bear's shirt.
7. Draw a pair of red birds in the sky.
8. Give the bear a pair of yellow earrings.
9. Draw a pair of brown shoes on the bear.
10. Draw a pair of green stars on the bear's pants.
11. Draw a pair of black pockets on the bear's shirt.
12. Give the bear a pair of apples in one of her hands.
13. Draw a pair of black snakes on the ground.
14. Draw a pair of patches on the bear's pants.
15. The bear is wearing something she wouldn't wear on a warm day in May. Put an X on this pair.

You dressed this bear very nicely!

Dress-a-Bear

Name ______________________________

A Day at the Zoo

Directions: Cut apart the pictures of the zoo animals on the next five pages. Then, encourage the children to listen carefully as you read the story below. After you read the story, ask the children the questions listed at the bottom of the page.

Brennan was very excited. His class was going on a field trip to the zoo. It was going to be a great day because they would get to see a lot of animals!

When the class got to the zoo, the first thing they saw was a giraffe. Its neck was very long!

Next, they saw two zebras. Brennan loved their black and white stripes.

Three elephants were in the next cage. They were spraying each other with water.

There were four slippery seals in the next cage.

After the seals, there were five alligators. Boy, they had a lot of teeth!

Next, there were six lions. One lion had a big mane of hair around its head.

Seven monkeys were swinging from a tree and eating bananas in the next cage.

There were eight penguins in the cage after the monkeys.

In the next cage, there were nine colorful birds.

In the last cage, there were snakes — ten of them!

Everyone in Brennan's class enjoyed the field trip to the zoo. When Brennan got home, he decided to draw pictures of all the animals he had seen. Here are the pictures he drew. (Show the pictures of the animals.) Let's help Brennan by writing the number of animals in each cage. (Have the children take turns counting the animals in each cage and writing that number in the box in the picture.)

Now, let's help Brennan put the cages in the order he saw them. What animal did he see first? (Help the children place the cages in the correct order.)

Super work! Brennan is glad you could help him!

Questions:

1. What did Brennan see right before he saw two zebras?
2. What did Brennan see right before he saw four seals?
3. What did Brennan see right after he saw six lions?
4. What did Brennan see right before he saw nine birds?
5. What did Brennan see right after he saw nine birds?

A Day at the Zoo, continued

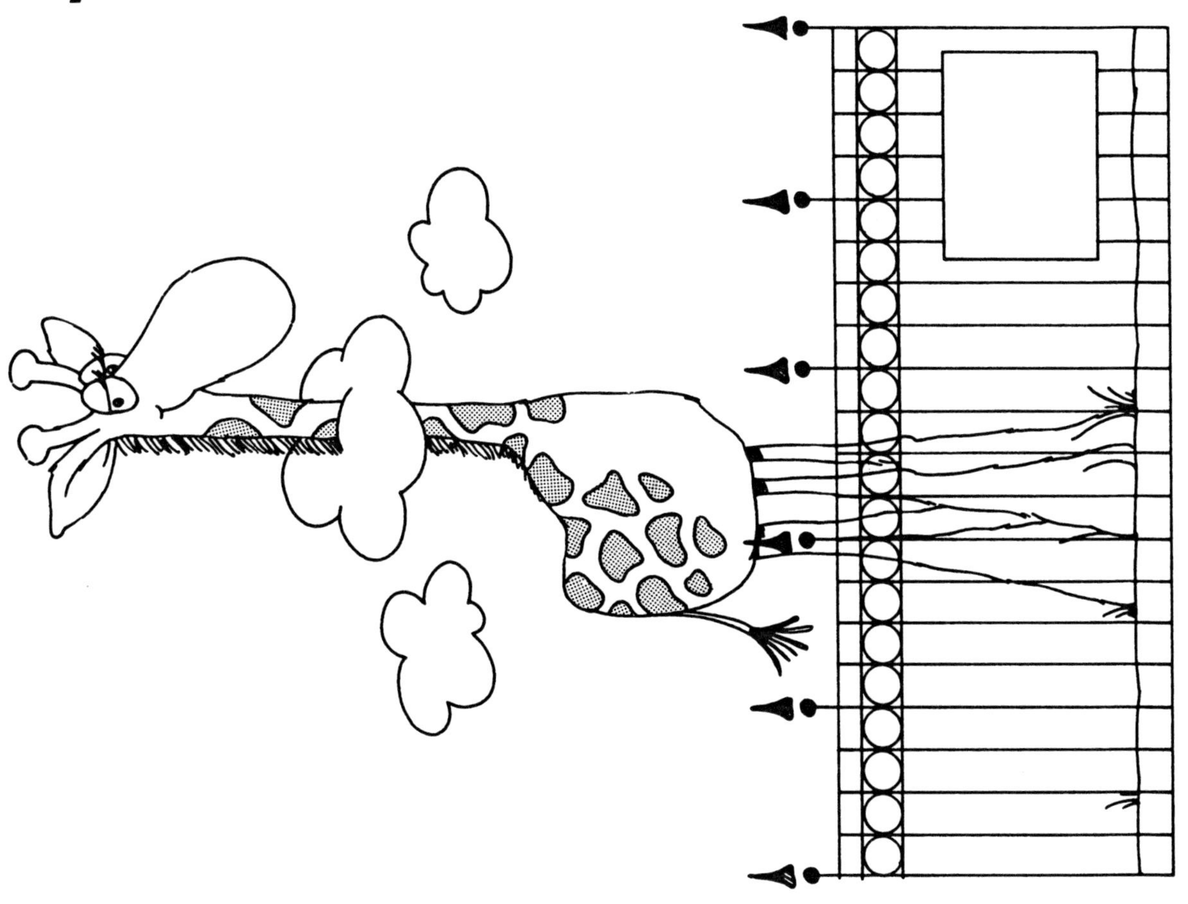

A Day at the Zoo, continued

A Day at the Zoo, continued

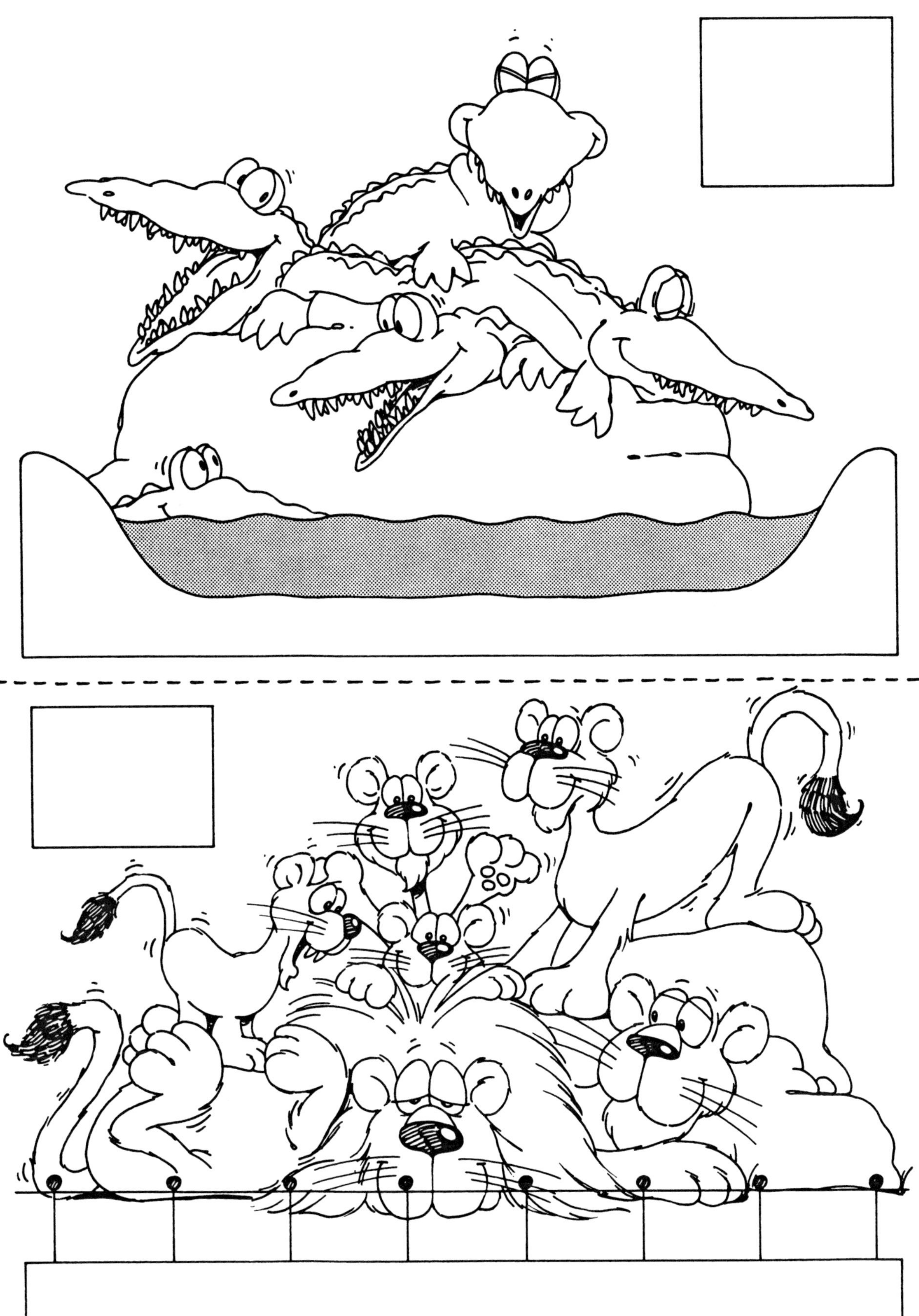

A Day at the Zoo, continued

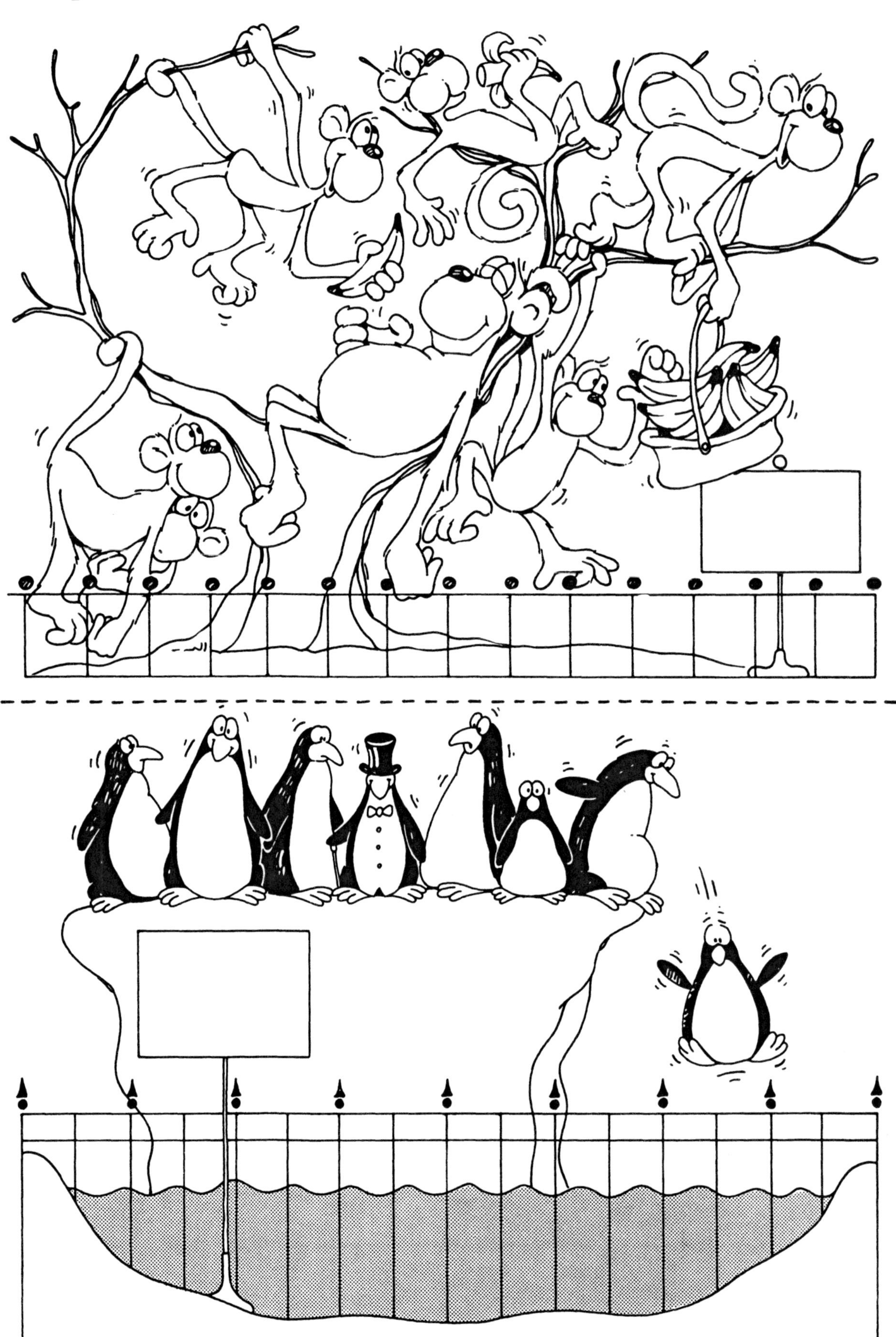

A Day at the Zoo, continued

Fun with Numbers: Instructions

Give each child a copy of *Fun with Numbers*.
Have the children listen carefully and follow
your directions.

1. What number comes after 1? Color that number black.
2. What number comes before 2? Put a purple X on that number.
3. What box has zero bears in it? Draw a green heart in that box.
4. What number comes after 9? Draw a green circle around that number.
5. What number comes before 8? Color that number orange.
6. What number tells how many wheels are on a car? Put a yellow X on that number.
7. What number comes before 4? Color that number red.
8. What number comes after 5? Put a red heart around that number.
9. What number comes before 6? Color that number blue.
10. What number comes before 9? Draw a brown line through that number.
11. What number comes after 8? Draw a yellow circle around that number.
12. What number shows how old you are? Draw a purple circle around that number.

There sure are a lot of bears on this page!

Fun with Numbers

Name ______________________

May: *number order and recognition*

What Are You Like?

Directions: Have the children line up in the room or outside. Tell the children you want to find out a little bit about each of them by playing a game. Tell them to listen carefully and follow your directions.

For additional practice, have the children make up directions using the words *no* and *not* to find out more about each other.

1. If you like school, stand on your tiptoes. If you do not like school, sit down.
2. If you live on a farm, shake your right arm. If you do not live on a farm, shake your left arm.
3. If you have no shoes, touch your nose. If you have shoes, touch your toes.
4. If you like ice cream, lick your lips. If you do not like ice cream, close your eyes.
5. If you like candy, rub your tummy. If you do not like candy, put your hands on your head.
6. If you do not like to swim, fold your arms in front of you. If you like to swim, put your hands up in the air.
7. If you have any sisters, touch your toes. If you have no sisters, touch your knees.
8. If you have a beard, touch your chin. If you do not have a beard, sit down.
9. If you like vegetables, clap five times. If you do not like vegetables, clap one time.
10. If you do not like summer vacation, make a mad face. If you like summer vacation, smile.
11. If you do not have a remote control car, sit down. If you have a remote control car, clap your hands once.
12. If you have a bicycle, stomp your feet on the floor. If you have no bicycle, take two steps forward.
13. If you do not like to sing, cover your mouth with your hands. If you like to sing, pretend you're singing.
14. If you are the only child in your family, sit down. If you are not the only child in your family, do a jumping jack.
15. If you have no front teeth, stick your tongue out. If you have front teeth, show me a big smile.

Play Ball: Instructions

Give each child a copy of *Play Ball*. Have the children listen carefully and follow your directions. Remind them to listen for the words *no* and *not*.

1. Color the baseball bat brown, but do not color the tape on the handle.
2. Find the baseball that has no hat. Draw a yellow hat on that baseball.
3. Find the baseball that does not have freckles. Give that baseball some orange freckles.
4. Find the ball that is not a baseball. Color that ball brown.
5. Find the baseballs that have no bow ties. Give each of those baseballs a red bow tie.
6. Find the ball that has no mouth. Draw a smiley face on that baseball.
7. Color Brennan's shirt blue, but do not color the buttons.
8. Find the ball that is not happy. Color that ball blue.
9. Find the baseball with no nose. Give that baseball a black nose.
10. Color Brennan's pants yellow, but do not color the pockets.
11. Find something that is not a ball and draw a green circle around it.
12. Find the baseballs that are not inside the baseball diamond. Draw a black line under each of those baseballs.
13. Find the bases Brennan is not standing on. Color those bases brown.
14. Color all the hats on the baseballs, but do not color any of them blue.
15. Draw a purple circle around each ball that is not sad.

What sports can we play with these balls?

Play Ball

Name ______________________________

BABE

May: *no, not*

The Grizzly Express

Directions: Encourage the children to listen carefully as you read the story below. Remind them to listen for the words *beginning*, *middle*, and *end*. After you read the story, ask the children the questions listed at the bottom of the page.

Brennan loved trains, so one day his father took him to the train station to see the Grizzly Express train. A nice conductor showed them the train from beginning to end.

The conductor explained that the beginning of the train was called the engine. Brennan saw many buttons and switches in this car. The buttons and switches were used to run the train. The man who drove the train, the engineer, was in the engine, too. He let Brennan blow the big, loud whistle. Woo, woo!

In the middle of the train, there were many cars. There was a car that held all the people traveling in the train. This was called the passenger car. It had nice, soft seats and a little restaurant. The conductor told Brennan that this was the car where he gathered tickets from the people riding on the train.

There were also storage cars in the middle of the train. The storage cars carried food, cars, wood, and sometimes animals. "Wow," said Brennan. "A train is a busy place!"

At the end of the train, Brennan saw a red caboose. The caboose was the smallest car in the train. It had a bell to ring and two lights on the back. A man stood in the window and waved to Brennan. This was Brennan's favorite car because it was red and shiny!

Questions:

1. Where was the train engine?
2. What did Brennan see in the train engine?
3. Tell who worked in the beginning car.
4. Where was the passenger car?
5. What other cars were in the middle of the train?
6. Who worked in the middle car?
7. Where were the animals, food, and cars carried?
8. Where was the caboose?
9. Tell what the caboose looked like.
10. Which was Brennan's favorite train car?

Brennan's Garden: Instructions

Give each child a copy of *Brennan's Garden*. Have the children listen carefully and follow your directions. Remind them to listen for the words *beginning*, *middle*, and *end*.

1. Draw an orange carrot at the beginning of the garden.
2. Draw a brown potato at the end of the garden.
3. Draw two purple flowers in the middle of the garden.
4. Draw a red radish at the end of the garden.
5. If the butterfly is near the middle of the garden, color it blue and yellow. If the butterfly is near the beginning of the garden, color it purple and orange.
6. Draw a big, yellow sun in the middle of the sky.
7. Draw a green head of lettuce at the beginning of the garden.
8. Draw a green pea pod at the end of the garden.
9. Draw a yellow squash in the middle of the garden.
10. Draw an orange pumpkin at the end of the garden.
11. Draw a yellow ear of corn at the beginning of the garden.
12. Draw a blue flower in the middle of the garden.
13. If the ladybug is at the end of the garden, color it red. If the ladybug is at the beginning of the garden, color it brown.
14. Draw one yellow ear of corn in the middle of the garden.
15. Draw an orange flower at the beginning of the garden.

Which part of the garden has the most vegetables?

Brennan's Garden

Name ______________________

May: *beginning, middle, end*

Brennan's Bad Day

Directions: Encourage the children to listen carefully as you read the story below. Remind them to listen for the word *starting*. After you read the story, ask the children the questions listed at the bottom of the page.

It was track day at school and Brennan was very excited. He was going to be in three events — running, jumping, and throwing. "I hope I win three ribbons," thought Brennan. "Then, I'll win the big trophy of the day!"

The first event was a race. "On your marks, get set, go!" Brennan was just starting to run when his feet got tangled up and he fell down. He got up and wiped the dirt off his knees just in time to see Dennis Dog cross the finish line. Brennan was disappointed, but he ran up to Dennis and shook his paw. "Congratulations! You're the fastest animal in the school," said Brennan.

"Thanks," said Dennis. "It must be from chasing all those mail carriers."

The second event was the high jump. When it was Brennan's turn, he ran up to the bar and was starting to jump when he suddenly slipped on a banana peel and ran right into the bar. "Oh, dear," said Brennan. "I'm having a bad day!"

Betty Bunny won the high jump and Brennan was happy for her. "Nice work, Betty," said Brennan. "You sure have strong jumping legs!"

The last event was the softball throw. As Brennan was starting to throw, he felt a terrible pain in his arm — he had pulled a muscle. The ball fell from his hand and rolled two feet away. "Oh, bummer!" said Brennan.

Bernie Bear won the softball throw and Brennan was glad for him. "Super job," said Brennan. "You're a great thrower!"

Finally, it was time to pass out the awards. Bernie won the big trophy because he scored the most points. "Oh, well," thought Brennan. "I had a bad day!"

Suddenly, Brennan heard his name over the loudspeaker. "Brennan Bear is the winner of the Best Sport Trophy," the voice said. "Even though he had some bad luck today, he was happy for everyone else who won. Let's hear it for Brennan!"

Brennan came up and got his trophy. Maybe it wasn't such a bad day after all!

Questions:

1. What was happening at Brennan's school?
2. Name the three events Brennan entered.
3. Who was the fastest animal in the school?
4. How did Brennan lose the high jump event?
5. What was the last event of the day?
6. Tell who won the softball throw.
7. Why did Brennan win the Best Sport Trophy?
8. Tell what kind of day Brennan had.

Track Meet: Instructions

Give each child a copy of *Track Meet*. Have the children listen carefully and follow your directions. Remind them to listen for the word *starting*.

Look at row one.

1. Color the bear who is starting to run brown.
2. Put a red X on the bear who is running.
3. Draw a green circle around the bear who finished running.

Look at row two.

1. Color the bear who is jumping black.
2. Color the shoes of the bear who is finished jumping blue.
3. Draw a yellow line under the bear who is starting to jump.

Look at row three.

1. Color the bear who is finished throwing orange.
2. Find the bear who is starting to throw. Color his uniform purple.
3. Find the bear who is throwing. Draw a red X on that bear.

Look at row four.

1. Find the bear who is starting to jump. Color that bear's uniform red and blue.
2. Find the bear who is jumping. Give that bear red shoes.
3. Find the bear who is finished jumping. Give that bear yellow shoes.

Look at row five.

1. Find the bear who is finished throwing. Draw an orange circle around that bear.
2. Color the bear who is starting to throw blue.
3. Draw a black box around the bear who is throwing.

What a great day for a track meet!

Track Meet

Name ______________________

Home Lesson

Dear ________________,

During the month of May, we have been working on these concepts: *pair*, *number order and recognition*, *no*, *not*, *beginning*, *middle*, *end*, and *starting*. You can help your child review these concepts by giving your child the sheet attached to this page.

Read the directions below and encourage your child to listen carefully and follow your directions. Here are the materials you will need: a box of eight crayons, a table, a chair, and a quiet place to work.

Directions:

1. Draw a pair of blue clouds in the sky.
2. Give the animal that is not a bear or a squirrel a red baseball cap.
3. What letter is at the beginning of your first name? Write that letter on the squirrel's shirt.
4. What number comes after 6? Write that number on the bear's shirt.
5. Draw a pair of red birds in one of the trees.
6. Draw a blue fish in the middle of the pond.
7. Draw a brown fish on the end of the rabbit's fishing line.
8. What number comes before 5? Write that number on the rabbit's shirt.
9. Draw two green leaves on the stem of the flower that has no leaves.
10. Give the bear a pair of orange glasses.
11. If you are a grown-up, draw three stars in the sky. If you are not a grown-up, draw a yellow sun in the sky.
12. Color the middle lily pad green.
13. What number comes after 2? Draw that many apples in the tree that has no birds.
14. Draw a green leaf starting to fall from one of the trees.

Have a fun and happy summer!

Sincerely,

____

Name ____________________

Spring Concept Check

Directions: Use this concept check to see how well your children remember the concepts they've learned in the past few months. Give each child the following page. Then, have the children listen carefully and follow your directions.

1. Color the clouds that are in a row blue. Put a purple X on the other clouds.
2. Color the first duck on the bench red. Color the next duck brown. Color the last duck blue.
3. Look at the nest in the tree.

   Find the egg that shows before a chick hatches. Color the egg yellow.
   Find the egg that shows after a chick hatched. Color the egg green.
4. How many fish are in the pond? Draw an equal number of apples in the tree with the nest.
5. Color some, but not many of the leaves green.
6. Find the two clouds that match. Draw a yellow circle around each cloud.
7. Look at the jars of worms.

   Color the jar that's almost empty brown.
   Draw a yellow circle around the jar that's full of worms.
8. Color the flowers that are together purple.
9. Use an orange crayon to color the flowers that are separated by a tree.
10. How many frogs are there? Draw the same number of yellow butterflies.
11. Color the pair of rabbits brown.
12. Find the bear who does not have any fish. Color that bear's shirt red.
13. Find the bear who is starting to fish. Color that bear brown.
14. Look at the ducks in the sky.

    Draw a black circle around the duck at the beginning.
    Draw an orange circle around the duck at the end.
    Draw a blue circle around the duck in the middle.
15. Find the tree with no apples. Color the tree trunk brown.
16. Color several of the frogs brown.
17. What number comes before 3? Draw that many clouds in the sky.
18. Put a black X on as many fish as there are bears on this page.

I'm proud of you for all your hard work!

Name ______________________

1-13-26